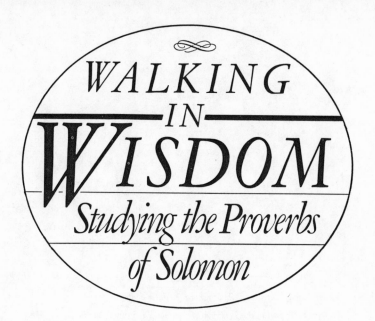

WALKING
—IN—
WISDOM
Studying the Proverbs
of Solomon

WILLIAM E. MOUSER, JR.

D0096149

InterVarsity Press
Downers Grove
Illinois 60515

InterVarsity Press is the book-publishing division of Inter-Varsity Christian Fellowship, a student movement active on campus at hundreds of universities, colleges and schools of nursing. For information about local and regional activities, write IVCF, 233 Langdon St., Madison, WI 53703.

Distributed in Canada through InterVarsity Press, 860 Denison St., Unit 3, Markham, Ontario L3R 4H1, Canada.

All Scripture quotations, unless otherwise indicated, are from the New American Standard Bible, © The Lockman Foundation 1960, 1962, 1963, 1968, 1971, 1972, 1973, 1975, 1977, and are used by permission.

Cover photograph: Robert McKendrick

ISBN 0-87784-846-7

Printed in the United States of America

Library of Congress Cataloging in Publications Data

Mouser, William E., 1947-
    Walking in wisdom.

    1. Bible. O.T. Proverbs–Criticism, interpreta-
tion, etc. I. Title.
BS1465.2.M68   1983   223'.706   83-265
ISBN 0-87784-846-7

19	18	17	16	15	14	13	12	11	10	9	8	7	6	5	4	3	2	1
97	96	95	94	93	92	91	90	89	88	87	86	85	84	83				

Dedicated to
Ernie and Vonita Mouser,
wise parents who
taught me to love
wisdom.

[CHAPTER ONE]

What Is a Proverb?

IF YOU WERE TO WALK INTO A hotel room anywhere in the world and look for the phone book, you would have no trouble finding it. Even if you do not speak a word of the language in which it is written, the phone book is identifiable by various characteristics you immediately recognize. It is probably the largest book in the room, especially if you are in a metropolitan area. When you open it, you see it is composed almost exclusively of lists—columns of words paired with numbers. If a Roman alphabet is employed, the words are alphabetized. Phone books are very similar to one another in any language.

You might easily recognize other literature of a language you do not speak. Poetry, for example, often takes specific forms—brief lines in groups numbering two or three to several dozen. Stanzas are separated by extra space on the page.

In our own language we can distinguish among many kinds of literature. Almost without thinking, we can tell the difference between fiction and nonfiction, prose and poetry, reference works and narratives, songs and sagas, cookbooks and concordances, merely on the basis of distinctive traits these forms of literature have. After reading the words "Once upon a time," we know immediately what *kind* of literature is going to follow.

A proverb can be recognized by various characteristics also. "An oak tree, though it is very large, began its life as an acorn." This sentence might have been spoken during a lecture on elementary botany. "Mighty oaks from little acorns grow." This is a proverb.

Characteristics of a Proverb

Solomon's proverbs display characteristics which set them off from most other nonbiblical proverbs. They are almost always composed of two thoughts brought together in various parallelisms. Solomon's proverbs frequently make highly imaginative use of figures of speech. In spite of their peculiar features, however, Solomon's proverbs share several basic characteristics with all other proverbs.

The most basic characteristics of a proverb can be observed by considering a very common proverb, "Like father, like son." This proverb occurs in almost every language in the world. It appears in the Bible in the form "Like mother, like daughter" (Ezek 16:44). By reflecting on this proverb, several characteristics of a proverb become evident.

A proverb is brief. Proverbs of more than twenty-five words are uncommon. If more words than this are employed, the text begins to sound like a parable. The very best proverbs are those which say the most in the fewest words. "Like father, like son" excels in brevity.

The brevity of a proverb arises partly from an artistic effort to express the most wisdom in the fewest words. Brevity also makes a proverb easier to remember. If, as is often the case, a proverb displays some word play, symmetry, euphony or striking image, then memorizing it becomes almost automatic.

A proverb is concrete. The origin of the proverb "Like father, like son" is easy to imagine. That origin is still with us—fathers and sons look alike. "He's a chip off the old block" speaks to the same point, but it uses a different concrete image—a chip of wood taken from a larger block. Since the dawn of creation, things have continued to beget after their own kind.

Most proverbs probably had their origin in some concrete aspect of human living. Wisdom sayings that move very far from concrete images and pictures begin to sound flat or trite. On the other hand, proverbs which paint vivid concrete pictures retain a freshness which makes them easy to recall.

In 1 Samuel 10 we can see a proverb crystallize from a concrete event in King Saul's early life. As the prophet Samuel had promised, Saul met a band of prophets after Samuel had anointed him king over Israel. When the Spirit of God came upon him, Saul prophesied with the prophets. Those who knew Saul were amazed; prophesying with the prophets was an activity far out of character for Saul. So the onlookers expressed their amazement with the question "Is Saul among the prophets?" This question became a proverb. When someone wished to express the idea that a fellow was acting out of character, he would say, "Is Saul among the prophets?"

A proverb is a general truth. "Like father, like son" tells us little if it merely asserts physical similarity between fathers and sons. The proverb escapes triviality because its concrete assertion is actually an embodiment of a general rule. "Like father, like son" functions as many proverbs do, uniting general patterns, rules or paradigms of living with specific examples of those patterns. The physical resemblance between fathers and sons can be seen in a glance. It might take much longer to observe the intangible things which fathers and sons share—common values, priorities, goals, likes and dislikes, character strengths and weaknesses. Not only do proverbs embody general rules in specific examples, but they also express intangible, spiritual truths through concrete assertions.

Indeed, sons act like their fathers far more often than they look like them. Sons may resemble their fathers' physical appearance in minor ways—hair coloring, skin tone or skeletal structure. But sons inherit large portions of their fathers' character. A son's spiritual inheritance from his father is more pervasive than his biological inheritance.

However, if we reflect a moment we might recall some son who not only fails to look like his father but also does not act like him. Does this prove the proverb to be incorrect? No, for proverbs are generalizations drawn from experience. The exceptional, the unusual, the unprecedented, all these are beyond the range of proverbial wisdom.

Proverbs have diverse applications. If many proverbs are general principles embodied in a concrete example, it is not surprising to find proverbs having diverse applications. For example, "Like father, like son" is true in contexts other than family relationships.

Consider for a moment *why* "Like father, like son" is a generally true statement. Children learn largely by mimicking. They almost instinctively watch their parents and copy what they see their parents do. Even when a child does not mimic his parents' behavior (say, for example, in eating spinach), the parent will often impose that behavior ("Johnny, eat that spinach or you'll get a spanking"). If the parents are only moderately successful in training their child, the child will leave the home with far more than his family's taste in vegetables; he will leave thoroughly imbued with his family's *character*.

For this reason, "Like father, like son" bears upon relationships which share similarities with the family relationship of parent and child. "Like teacher, like pupil," "Like pastor, like congregation," "Like coach, like athlete" would be possible variants. To the degree that the relationships of teacher-pupil, pastor-congregation or coach-athlete share common features of the father-son relationship, then "Like father, like son" will speak something true of them.

What Proverbs Are Not
The characteristic of a proverb which most people would mention first is its brevity. Any dictionary defines a proverb as a "pithy saying." In addition to this feature, we have seen how a proverb often arises from some concrete fact or event in daily living. A proverb then comes to express a general rule through a specific example. These characteristics distinguish proverbs from other kinds of literature.

Some Christians, therefore, make a basic interpretive mistake when they understand Solomon's proverbs as some other kind of literature. The two kinds of literature most often confused with proverbial literature are *laws* and *promises*.

Some Christians read the proverbs as if they were inflexible laws of God's creation, admitting no exceptions. A casual reading of almost any chapter in Solomon's proverbs will yield an abundance of proverbs which have exceptions. The book of Proverbs does not encourage us to read its contents as inflexible laws. Consider, for example, Proverbs 26:4-5:

Do not answer a fool according to his folly,
Lest you also be like him.
Answer a fool as his folly deserves,
Lest he be wise in his own eyes.

Some fools we answer and some we do not, if we are wise. Proverbial wisdom will always have a problematic dimension because the world in which we live is fallen, full of uncertainties and unpredictable in many ways. Proverbial wisdom isolates and names the underlying patterns and principles which abide more or less constant in the flux of human living.

Christians will also sometimes confuse proverbs with promises. Because the proverbs of Solomon are Scripture, it is supposed that God himself will guarantee the performance of every proverb. This has put a strain on many Christians' faith when they have "claimed God's promises in prayer," holding up some proverb to God. When the exceptional or the unusual occurs, they then think God has failed to fulfill his promise. However, proverbs in Solomon's collection are not promises made by God, but are guides which are to direct people in living successful and productive lives.

What Are the Proverbs of Solomon?
Proverbs 1:1 contains the title of the book: "The proverbs of Solomon . . . king of Israel." What then are we to think when we read "the proverbs of Solomon" at Proverbs 10:1? Such a notice looks very much like a subheading, indicating that at 10:1 we are to find the proverbs proper. If this is correct, then we might conclude that what precedes Proverbs 10:1 are not proverbs.

In this conclusion we would be correct. The traits of proverbs discussed previously do not correspond at all with the material in Proverbs 1—9. In these chapters we find paternal exhortations delivered to a son to encourage his pursuit of wisdom. The father frequently addresses his son (Prov 2:1; 3:1; 4:1; 5:1; 6:1). A proverb is not a promise, yet there are many promises in Proverbs 1—9 relative to the acquisition of wisdom. While these chapters include much by way of moral instruction (for example, chapters 5—7), this instruction comes from a father rather than from a student's meditation on a proverb. The father of Proverbs 1—9 exhorts his son to pursue wisdom, promises him success in living for doing so and warns him of calamity should he fail to become wise.

The book you are reading will aid you in beginning an

enjoyable and profitable lifetime study of Proverbs. What is said in later chapters about figures of speech and parallelisms in Hebrew poetry and proverbs can also be easily and fruitfully applied to other poetry in the English Bible.

Study Questions: Chapter One

1. Below are various statements taken from the Old and New Testaments. Some are proverbs, some are promises, and some are commandments or laws. Without looking up the context of each statement, determine whether it is a proverb, promise or law/commandment.

☐ You shall not muzzle the ox while he is threshing. (Deut 25:4)

☐ Let us eat and drink, for tomorrow we die. (1 Cor 15:32)

☐ Love your enemies, and pray for those who persecute you. (Mt 5:44)

☐ I will never desert you, nor will I ever forsake you. (Heb 13:5)

☐ If a man steals an ox or a sheep, and slaughters it or sells it, he shall pay five oxen for the ox and four sheep for the sheep. (Ex 22:1)

☐ Bad company corrupts good morals. (1 Cor 15:33)

☐ The stranger who resides with you shall be to you as the native among you, and you shall love him as yourself. (Lev 19:34)

☐ If we confess our sins, He is faithful and righteous to forgive us our sins and to cleanse us from all unrighteousness. (1 Jn 1:9)

☐ The fathers eat the sour grapes, but the children's teeth are set on edge. (Ezek 18:2)

☐ Those who wait for the LORD will gain new strength; they will mount up with wings like eagles, they will run and not get tired, they will walk and not become weary. (Is 40:31)

☐ A single witness shall not rise up against a man on account of any iniquity or any sin which he has committed; on the evidence of two or three witnesses a matter shall be confirmed. (Deut 19:15)

☐ Physician, heal yourself! (Lk 4:23)

☐ Keep aloof from every brother who leads an unruly life and not according to the tradition which you received from us. (2 Thess 3:6)

☐ Wherever the corpse is, there the vultures will gather (Mt 24:28)

☐ Whoever will call upon the name of the Lord will be saved. (Rom 10:13)

☐ Out of the wicked comes forth wickedness. (1 Sam 24:13)

☐ Honor your father and your mother, that your days may be prolonged in the land the LORD your God gives you. (Ex 20:12)

2. For each of the statements you have identified as proverbs, indicate briefly which of the four characteristics of proverbs are displayed—brevity, concreteness, generality, diversity of application.

[CHAPTER TWO]

Why Meditate on a Proverb?

SOME PEOPLE WHO ARE AFFLICTED with mild wakefulness read their phone books. Merely half a page of the A's or the H's is almost certain to produce drowsiness. It would be comical, however, to suppose that the telephone company wrote their book in order to cure mild insomnia in their customers. A phone book may be used not only to induce sleep, but it may also be used to prop open a door, to swat flies (a smallish phone book is best) or to place under Baby so that he can sit comfortably at the table (a rather largish phone book is best). When a phone book is used in these ways, the user is deliberately ignoring the purpose which the authors of the phone book had in mind when they compiled it.

There is no great harm, perhaps, in ignoring the purpose of a phone book when using it to various ends. However, several decades ago thousands of Americans were sent into panic when they heard on their radios that the Martians had landed and were handily defeating all who tried to oppose them. The frightened listeners had tuned in late and had missed hearing that a radio dramatization of H. G. Wells's *War of the Worlds* was being broadcast. They heard the broadcaster's words as if his purpose were "to report an invasion from Mars." His real purpose, of course, was "to entertain our listeners with a dramatization of a popular work of science fiction." Ignorance of the author's purpose in the radio broadcast led to serious misunderstanding.

We may avoid similar misunderstanding by taking seriously the purpose of any book we read. J. Sidlow Baxter once noted that Leviticus yields little if merely read, but it yields much when carefully studied. The same could be said for the genealogies of Genesis and 1 Chronicles, the collections of laws in Exodus and Deuteronomy, as well as nonbiblical books such as cookbooks and phone books. Collections— whether they be collections of names, recipes, regulations for sacrifices, compilations of laws or collections of hymns like the book of Psalms—are almost never intended by their authors to be read from beginning to end. Only one of the elements of the collection is ordinarily of interest to a reader at one time.

The book of Proverbs is a collection. Solomon spoke 3,000 proverbs (1 Kings 4:32). Approximately 300 of these are collected in Proverbs 10:1—22:16. After these come "the words of the wise" (Prov 22:17—24:22) and "sayings of the wise" (Prov 24:23-34). King Hezekiah's scribes added about 130 more Solomonic proverbs (Prov 25:1—29:27). Then come the words of Agur (Prov 30:1-33), the words of King Lemuel (Prov 31:1-9) and the acrostic poem on the virtuous wife (Prov 31:10-31).

The title of the collection is found in Proverbs 1:1: "The proverbs of Solomon... king of Israel." Immediately after this title, in verses 2-5, the purpose of the entire collection is specified. A close examination of this purpose is mandatory if we are to use the collection accurately and profitably.

The Dual Purpose of Solomon's Proverbs

Normal Hebrew style states an idea in summary form and then restates the idea more elaborately. Thus the purpose of the book of Proverbs is summarized in Proverbs 1:2: "To know wisdom and instruction,/To discern the sayings of understanding." Though these purposes are elaborated in verses 3-6, the purposes of Solomon's collection of proverbs are basically two.

The first purpose of Solomon's collection—to know wisdom and instruction—is somewhat obscure in our English versions. The Hebrew verb "to know," *yada'*, is very flexible in its meanings. Often it takes its significance from the things which are said to be known or the circumstances in which the knowing occurs. To know one's wife, for example, means to make love to her (Gen 4:1). To know hunting means to be a skillful hunter (Gen 25:57). To know books means to be literate (Is 29:11).

Wisdom in Hebrew corresponds best to our notion of "skill," a practical proficiency in performance. *Instruction* in Proverbs 1:2 means "discipline," the kind of activity in which a father trains up a son, possibly quite rigorous activity (compare Deut 8:2-5!). So, *to know wisdom and instruction* probably means something like "to acquire living skills and moral discipline." The emphasis of this purpose of Solomon's proverbs is more moral than mental, focusing on the character rather than the mind. The practical skills to live successfully and the moral discipline to learn and implement those skills are the things which the proverbs are designed to impart to the reader.

The mental development of the reader, however, is not overlooked. The second purpose of Solomon's proverbs mentioned in Proverbs 1:2 is "to discern the sayings of understanding." The verb *discern* means to distinguish between things, primarily between right and wrong, wisdom and folly, uprightness and perverseness. Solomon's prayer in 1 Kings 3:9 uses the same vocabulary: "Give Thy servant an understanding heart to judge Thy people to discern between good and evil."

Solomon's Moral Purpose Expanded

After specifying the purpose of his collection in summary form, Solomon elaborates these purposes in the following four verses. The first three verses restate the moral purpose of Solomon's proverbs from three different perspectives.

The perspective of a student is first considered. For the student, the purpose of Solomon's proverbs is "to receive instruction in wise behavior, righteousness, justice and equity." *Wise behavior* is one word in Hebrew, and it means "prudence." The word is applied to Abigail in 1 Samuel 25:3, and her actions in that chapter provide a concrete example of the virtue which the student of Proverbs is to receive.

The English versions all read as if there were four things which the student is to receive: wise behavior, righteousness, justice and equity. However, the translators have failed to note the Massoretic punctuation of this verse, which indicates that the last three terms are adverbial accusatives indicating the manner in which the wise behavior is to be manifested. The paraphrase in the Living Bible captures the sense: "How to act in every circumstance, for he wanted them to be understanding, just and fair in everything they did." It is possible, of course, to receive wisdom in wickedness. Satan himself is very wise (Gen 3:1; 2 Cor 11:3). But Solomon says that the student of his proverbs will receive only that prudence which issues in righteousness, justice and equity.

The perspective of the teacher is considered in Proverbs 1:4. The proverbs are not for the reclusive sage but for the skillful teacher. Though the naive and the foolish share many characteristics, there is hope for the naive. The folly of the naive is that of the untrained, untaught youth. To live skillfully, they must be taught wisdom and discretion. This is the goal and purpose of the proverbs in the hands of a teacher of wisdom —to take the naive and give them prudence, knowledge and discretion.

The perspective of the wise man is adopted in Proverbs 1:5. The moral purpose of Solomon's proverbs has not been completed when we become wise from meditating on them and incorporating their wisdom into our lives. The wise can hear and increase still more in learning. Those of understanding can gain wise counsel beyond what they already possess.

Solomon's Mental Purpose Expanded
The verbs *discern* and *understand* in Proverbs 1:2b and 1:6 are identical in the Hebrew text, though they are translated by different words in the New American Standard Bible and in some other English versions. This suggests that the summary statement of purpose in 1:2b is being expanded in 1:6. Further evidence for seeing 1:6 as an expansion of the previously mentioned mental purpose of the proverbs is the similarity between "sayings of understanding" in 1:2b and the vocabulary of wisdom speech in 1:6—proverb, figure, words of the wise and riddles.

Proverbs and "words of the wise" are the elements that compose Solomon's collection of wisdom. Figures and riddles, on the other hand, are the stuff of proverbs and wise sayings. Solomon's proverbs often make elaborate and complex use of figures of speech; four chapters of this book are devoted to defining and illustrating such figures. Many of the proverbs are so crafted as to pose mental puzzles which require careful, discerning effort to unravel. The student who learns to discern figures of speech and unlock the riddles posed by many proverbs will develop a mental keenness and acumen which is valuable for any endeavor.

There appears to be a difficulty in the statement of the mental purpose of Solomon's proverbs. That a given book should have as its purpose the understanding of another book is a familiar notion. The purpose of this book, for example, is to help you understand the proverbs of Solomon. Likewise, one of the purposes of Solomon's proverbs is to teach us to understand his proverbs. Yet how can this be, since no section of the book of Proverbs explains how to understand a proverb?

The answer lies in Solomon's approach to the acquisition of wisdom and discernment. These virtues are not to be had by mere reading or even diligent study alone. *Learning by doing* is the primary way we develop mental and moral capacities. Some proverbs are very simple and transparent (for example, Prov 10:1; 19:26). Other proverbs are very obscure (for example, Prov 30:18-19). As you learn the speech of wisdom by progressing from the simple to the complex, your mental acumen will increase, not only toward understanding more difficult proverbs but also toward discerning accurately the words and works of those you encounter in day-to-day living.

The mental purpose of Solomon's proverbs is realized as you think about the proverbs. As you learned to walk by walking, so you can learn to be discerning by pondering the proverbs of Solomon. Mental skills can be attained through practice every bit as much as moral skills. Solomon's proverbs are intended to produce both.

Study Questions: Chapter Two

1. Though the book of Proverbs has a dual purpose, the moral and mental advancement of its students, some individual proverbs major on one of these purposes. Some proverbs are more riddles than bits of moral instruction; some are clearly aimed at developing moral rather than mental acumen. Read the following proverbs or section of proverbs and label each one as primarily *moral* or *mental* in its purpose for the student.

☐ The merciful man does himself good,
But the cruel man does himself harm. (11:17)

☐ There is one who scatters, yet increases all the more,
And there is one who withholds what is justly due, but it
results only in want. (11:24)

☐ A righteous man hates falsehood,
But a wicked man acts disgustingly and shamefully. (13:5)

☐ There is one who pretends to be rich, but has nothing;
Another pretends to be poor, but has great wealth. (13:7)

☐ Poverty and shame will come to him who neglects discipline,
But he who regards reproof will be honored. (13:18)

☐ A faithful witness will not lie,
But a false witness speaks lies. (14:5)

☐ The eyes of the LORD are in every place,
Watching the evil and the good. (15:3)

☐ Bright eyes gladden the heart;
Good news puts fat on the bones. (15:30)

☐ The king's wrath is like the roaring of a lion,
But his favor is like dew on the grass. (19:12)

☐ Listen to counsel and accept discipline,
That you may be wise the rest of your days. (19:20)

☐ He who assaults his father and drives his mother away
Is a shameful and disgraceful son. (19:26)

☐ Do not rob the poor because he is poor,
Or crush the afflicted at the gate;

For the LORD will plead their case,
And take the life of those who rob them. (22:22-23)
☐ Do not answer a fool according to his folly,
Lest you also be like him.
Answer a fool as his folly deserves,
Lest he be wise in his own eyes. (26:4-5)
☐ Iron sharpens iron,
So one man sharpens another. (27:17)
☐ A fool always loses his temper,
But a wise man holds it back. (29:11)
☐ An unjust man is abominable to the righteous,
And he who is upright in the way is abominable to the
    wicked. (29:27)
☐ There are three things which are too wonderful for me,
Four which I do not understand:
The way of an eagle in the sky,
The way of a serpent on a rock,
The way of a ship in the middle of the sea,
And the way of a man with a maid. (30:18-19)
2. Some of the moral teaching in Proverbs takes the form of
do's and don'ts (for example, Prov 22:17-29). The Ten Com-
mandments in Exodus 20 are also do's and don'ts, as are the
laws of Leviticus and Deuteronomy. How are these com-
mands of the Mosaic law different from those of Proverbs?

CHAPTER THREE

But & Both,
Either & Or:
Synonymous &
Antithetical Parallelisms

THE SMALLEST WORD IN BIBLICAL Hebrew is written with the next to the smallest letter of the Hebrew alphabet. The letter is *waw* and the word is *we*. Beginning Hebrew students are told that this word means "and," wherein begins much grief for the beginning Hebrew student. For, no sooner than he has mastered enough vocabulary to begin reading simple prose, he discovers that Hebrew composition seems to consist of stringing together simple clauses with *we* almost interminably. Every verse in Genesis 1 after the first verse begins with *we*. Even the books of Exodus, Leviticus, Numbers, Joshua, Judges, Ruth, 1 and 2 Samuel, and 1 and 2 Kings all begin with *we*.

At this point the Hebrew instructor begins to overload the poor student's linguistic circuitry. He tells the befuddled student that *we* does not mean "and." It only means "and" sometimes. When the confused student objects, "But, sir, ..." the instructor responds with "You are quite right. W^e sometimes means 'but.' It can also mean 'also'; or it can mean 'or.' If two of them are placed just so, they can mean 'either' and 'or.' "

So when the beginning Hebrew student learns that w^e can also mean "so," "therefore," "thus," "that," "so that" and "now," he either gives up Hebrew as something exceedingly mysterious, or he concludes that w^e means nothing at all by itself; instead it gets its meaning solely from its context. In this conclusion the beginning student of Hebrew is exactly right.

The lexical ambiguity of w^e is adequately clarified by matters of context. After brief study in reading, a Hebrew student can wade through dozens of w^e's and get them all translated correctly. In King Solomon's hands, however, w^e becomes a puzzle. Most of Solomon's proverbs are *parallelisms*, pairs of statements laid alongside one another. Each member of a parallelism is parallel only to its partner. Most of the time these pairs of statements are joined together with a w^e. There is, however, no context. Each proverb stands by itself.

The initial problem confronting Solomon's original Hebrew-speaking audience was to figure out the sense of w^e. Did it mean "and," "but," "or," "so," or "thus"? For readers of Proverbs in English versions, this problem has often been solved by the translator. It is crucial, therefore, to know and understand the various kinds of parallelisms which the proverbs exhibit. In some cases you may need to correct the parallelism of the English version. Fortunately, you can learn to do so without learning biblical Hebrew.

Comparison and contrast are the most common rhetorical devices in the human language. The parallelisms of Solomon's proverbs make more use of these devices than any other. Each of these kinds of parallelisms is discussed in the following pages.

Synonymous Parallelisms

A proverb displays *synonymous parallelism* when the two ideas brought together are saying the same thing in different words. The second line will often repeat the first line in somewhat altered form in order to express the lesson of the proverb with maximum clarity. There may or may not be a conjunction; when there is a conjunction, it is translated "and." Proverbs 16:28, for example, has a conjunction:

> A perverse man spreads strife,
> And a slanderer separates intimate friends.

On the other hand, Proverbs 18:20 merely juxtaposes the synonymous sentences:

> With the fruit of a man's mouth his stomach will be satisfied;
> He will be satisfied with the product of his lips.

When a proverb exhibits synonymous parallelism, it is possible to omit part of one of the ideas because it is implied by the other idea. For example, in Proverbs 14:19 the verb is omitted from the second line:

> The evil will bow down before the good,
> And the wicked at the gates of the righteous.

The sense of the second line is clearly that "the wicked *will bow down* at the gates of the righteous," but the verb can be omitted because of the synonymous parallelism. In the same way, a subject may be omitted with the result that the proverb will read like a sentence with two predicates. Proverbs 18:18, for example, reads:

> The lot puts an end to contentions,
> And decides between the mighty.

In the examples cited so far, the synonymous parallelism was indicated by similar statements, even similar vocabulary between the two lines. However, some synonymous parallelisms can be identified only by attending to the whole ideas which are brought together. For example, consider Proverbs 10:23:

Doing wickedness is like sport to a fool;
And so is wisdom to a man of understanding.

The characters displayed to us are certainly contrasts—a fool and a man of understanding. Their activities are also contrasts—doing wickedness and doing wisdom. Nevertheless, the *ideas* of both are that this activity is sport for this person. Bringing these two lines together makes the point that the fool and the man of understanding have something in common after all: they each do something for the fun of it.

Proverbs 16:6 is another proverb in which the overall idea of the proverb must be considered in order to account for and identify the parallelism:

By lovingkindness and truth iniquity is atoned for,
And by the fear of the LORD one keeps away from evil.

The parallelism of this proverb is synonymous because each line is relating how one can deal with sin—it can be atoned for if already committed, or it can be avoided by the fear of the Lord.

Some synonymous parallelisms might be confused for parallelisms of contrast if the second line negates the contrast of some element in the first line. For example, Proverbs 12:28 reads:

In the way of righteousness is life,
And in its pathway there is no death.

As *death* and *life* are antonyms, the negation of *death* in the second line brings it into synonymous parallelism with the first line. Other examples of this are Proverbs 14:10 and 20:13:

The heart knows its own bitterness,
And a stranger does not share its joy.

Do not love sleep, lest you become poor;
Open your eyes, and you will be satisfied with food.

On the other hand, a proverb should not be identified as a

synonymous parallelism merely because its second line begins with *and*. Other parallelisms have second lines which begin with *and*, as for example, Proverbs 20:18:

Prepare plans by consultation,

And make war by wise guidance.

The phrases *by consultation* and *by wise guidance* are synonymous, but preparing plans is not synonymous with making war. Rather, the second line is applying to warfare the more general principle concerning making plans. This is a kind of *synthetic parallelism* (discussed in chapter six). In Proverbs 20:18, *we* would be better translated "so" or "therefore."

Another proverb where the second line begins with *and* in the English versions, yet which is not at all synonymous, is Proverbs 19:3:

The foolishness of man subverts his way,

And his heart rages against the LORD.

Therefore, the student should beware of identifying the parallelism of a given proverb merely by recourse to the conjunction *and*.

Antithetical Parallelism

A proverb displays *antithetical parallelism* when two ideas are contrasted with one another. Usually the two ideas are connected with a conjunction which is translated "but." In a few proverbs there is no conjunction, although the translator may supply *but* if he judges the parallelism to be antithetical.

For example, the first proverb of the collection beginning in 10:1 is an antithetical parallelism:

A wise son makes a father glad,

But a foolish son is a grief to his mother.

Proverbs 10:5 has the same symmetrical contrasts with no conjunction in the Hebrew text. In the English versions it has been supplied by the translator:

He who gathers in summer is a son who acts wisely;
But he who sleeps in harvest is a son who acts shamefully.

Just as with synonymous parallelisms, some antithetical parallelisms can only be identified by considering the whole idea of each line. For example, Proverbs 19:16 reads:

He who keeps the commandment keeps his soul,
But he who is careless of his ways will die.

The translator has supplied *but* appropriately, for the ideas in the two lines are being contrasted. The first line advises how to keep alive, while the second line warns about what will cause loss of life. It can also happen that one subject may have contrasting predicates instead of synonymous predicates. Proverbs 10:29 reads:

The way of the LORD is a stronghold to the upright,
But ruin to the workers of iniquity.

Just as the word *and* at the beginning of a second line does not invariably signal a synonymous parallelism, so the word *but* does not invariably indicate an antithetical parallelism. Proverbs 13:19 reads:

Desire realized is sweet to the soul,
But it is an abomination to fools to depart from evil.

If we ignore the *but* for a moment, we begin to see that the first line is giving a reason for the second line. This proverb is another synthetic parallelism. The Hebrew *we* which the translator has rendered "but" would be better translated "so": Desire realized is sweet to the soul; so it is an abomination to fools to depart from evil.

Similarly, Proverbs 17:3 is not antithetical. In translating it as if it were, the translators of the King James Version and the New American Standard Bible obscure the sense of the proverb:

The refining pot is for silver and the furnace for gold,
But the LORD tests the hearts.

The point of this proverb is to compare the work of the Lord in testing our hearts with the process of refining precious metals. By itself, the second line merely asserts that the Lord is an examiner. But when the comparison is made with refining precious metals, the point is made that the Lord's testing activity is intended to remove moral and spiritual dross from the heart in order to expose the pure qualities he values.

On the other hand, a few proverbs have a conjunction translated "and," even though the parallelism is antithetical. For example, Proverbs 14:17 reads:

A quick-tempered man acts foolishly,
And a man of evil devices is hated.

The actions of a quick-tempered man are not devised at all; they are spontaneous and unconsidered. For this reason, his actions are foolish. He is also the object of various condescending attitudes such as pity, derision or scorn. A man with a cool disposition, however, who calmly and carefully devises evil, earns not pity but enmity. The easily provoked man is laughed at and teased. The calculating villain is hated. The one only harms himself, whereas the other invites attack.

Only Practice Makes Perfect

There are other kinds of parallelisms in the proverbs besides those mentioned in this chapter, but those with parallelisms which either compare or contrast account for more than half the proverbs in the collection. It is just as important to be practiced in recognizing when a proverb is *not* synonymous or antithetical as it is to recognize these parallelisms when they occur. Some proverbs are so crafted that their parallelism is deliberately obscure. By learning to discern the more obvious antithetical and synonymous parallelisms, you will increase in the skills needed to clarify the more obscure proverbs.

You should beware of two things. First, never fail to test the "announced" form of parallelism in your English version. Antithetical parallelisms usually have *but* in the second line; synonymous parallelisms usually have *and*. However, either kind of parallelism may appear without any telltale conjunction, and occasionally the translator's interpretive decision may prove questionable.

Second, beware of deciding hastily the kind of parallelism a proverb displays. Solomon's proverbs were not posed as insoluble riddles; yet some of them are difficult. They often reveal their secrets only after considerable reflection. The more practiced you become, the less time you will need to spend in this exercise. However, it is an exercise which every student of Proverbs must perform, even the most advanced. Solomon's way to wisdom knows no short cuts. A speedier running of the course comes only after appropriate practice. Even then "a wise man will hear and increase in learning."

Study Questions: Chapter Three
1. Read each proverb in Proverbs 18:1-24 and classify each one as *(a)* synonymous parallelism, *(b)* antithetical parallelism, or *(c)* neither synonymous nor antithetical parallelism. Classify all the proverbs before checking your answers in the back of the book; you may want to change some of your classifications after you have had some practice.
2. Explain in a couple of sentences the difference in meaning between these two different translations of Proverbs 18:5.
☐ It is not good to accept the person of the wicked,
   to overthrow the righteous in judgment. (KJV)
☐ To show partiality to the wicked is not good,
   Nor to thrust aside the righteous in judgment. (NASB)
Which translation represents synonymous parallelism?
3. Read the following synonymous parallelisms and determine which of them contain one line which is a double negation of the idea in the other line. For example, Proverbs 12:28: In the way of righteousness is *life*,/And in its pathway there is *no death*.
☐ A false witness will not go unpunished,
   And he who tells lies will not escape. (19:5)
☐ Many will entreat the favor of a generous man,
   And every man is a friend to him who gives gifts. (19:6)
☐ A false witness will not go unpunished,
   And he who tells lies will perish. (19:9)
☐ Differing weights are an abomination to the LORD,
   And a false scale is not good. (20:23)
☐ Loyalty and truth preserve the king,
   And he upholds his throne by righteousness. (20:28)
☐ He who loves pleasure will become a poor man;
   He who loves wine and oil will not become rich. (21:17)

[CHAPTER FOUR]

Filling in the Blank: Asymmetrical Antithetical Parallelisms

ONE AND ONE IS MORE THAN TWO in Proverbs. By bringing two ideas together in a poetic parallelism, Solomon communicated more than the mere sum of the two ideas. The juxtaposition itself creates a puzzle. You must discern how the two ideas relate to one another, whether by contrast, comparison or some other relationship. In a synonymous parallelism, the message of the proverb gets fuller expression by being stated twice; in antithetical parallelisms, both the message and its converse are displayed.

In most of the parallelisms in Proverbs, either idea will stand by itself and make good sense. When you discern the relationship between the two ideas, then that relationship becomes a device for making inferences *about* one idea *from* the other idea *through* the relationship between them. Many of the proverbs, especially those which display antithetical parallelism, seem deliberately crafted so as to invite the making of inferences from the materials provided in the proverb. You must explicate what the proverb leaves unsaid through careful meditation on the elements of the proverb.

In order to recognize those proverbs which invite this kind of elaboration, you must first learn to identify those proverbs which invite no inferences at all—those antithetical parallelisms which display all their meaning on the surface. These proverbs are symmetrical contrasts and often are formally symmetrical as well.

Symmetrical Antithetical Parallelisms

A proverb exhibits symmetrical antithetical parallelism when the contrasts between the two ideas are all explicit in the words of the proverb. For example, consider Proverbs 10:1, the first proverb in Solomon's collection:

A wise son makes a father glad,
But a foolish son is a grief to his mother.

This proverb exhibits two kinds of symmetry which are clear from the following diagram:

10:1a	**10:1b**
a wise son	a foolish son
makes	is
a glad	a grief
father	mother

By means of a very slight paraphrasing of 10:1a, the formal symmetry can be seen in this diagram. Each line of the proverb follows the order of subject-verb-object; each subject is a noun modified by an adjective. The verbs are not precisely symmetrical, as one is transitive and the other intransitive; however, Proverbs often pairs transitive and intransitive verbs in both synonymous and antithetical parallelisms.

The other kind of symmetry displayed by Proverbs 10:1 involves the *sense* of each line. Each element in each line finds a precise lexical contrast in the other line. *Wise* and *foolish* contrast well with each other; *glad* and *grief* are opposite in sense even though they are not the same part of speech; even *father* and *mother* make an interesting counterpoint with one another even though they are not the same as the other contrasts in Proverbs 10:1. In both sense and form, Proverbs 10:1 is symmetrical.

Proverbs 15:1 is another symmetrical antithetical parallelism:

15:1a	**15:1b**
a gentle answer	a harsh word
turns away	stirs up
wrath	anger

The formal symmetry is evident in that each line follows the subject-verb-object pattern. The sense of Proverbs 15:1 is also symmetrical. *A gentle answer* is balanced with its contrast, *a harsh word*, and the verbs *turn away* and *stir up* also contrast well. *Wrath* and *anger*, of course, are synonyms. As we examine more antithetical parallelisms, it will become evident that they often contain synonymous elements on each side of the parallelism.

The symmetry of Proverbs 15:18 is easy to see when it is diagrammed:

15:18a	**15:18b**
a hot-tempered man	the slow to anger
stirs up	pacifies
strife	contention

The formal symmetry is not so rigid. The subjects, for example, are not the same form; 15:18a has a noun and an adjective for a subject, while the second line uses a substantive made from an adjective with an adverbial infinitive. Otherwise, the syntactical order of subject-verb-object is followed in each line of 15:18.

The sense of 15:18 is also symmetrical. Though the subjects are formally different, they are complete opposites in sense. *Stirs up* and *pacifies* make good contrasts as well. As we saw in the previous example, Proverbs 15:18 is an antithetical parallelism even though it contains the synonymous elements *strife* and *contention* paired in formal symmetry.

The formal symmetry which some antithetical parallelisms display can prove helpful in clarifying the sense of one or the other of the paired ideas. Consider, for example, the interpretive problem which pronouns pose in Proverbs 14:31:

He who oppresses the poor reproaches his Maker,
But he who is gracious to the needy honors Him.

If the second line is considered in isolation from the first, *honors him* could mean "honors the needy" (the Hebrew does not indicate whether *him* should be upper or lower case). Pairing the formal elements of the proverb, however, makes it clear that the actual antecedent of *him* is in the first line:

14:31a	14:31b
he who oppresses	he who is gracious
the poor	to the needy
reproaches	honors
his Maker	him

As *him* in 14:31b formally pairs with *his Maker* in 14:31a, they are probably synonymous terms, one being the antecedent of the other.

Notice that recourse to formal symmetry in 14:31 does not clear up the ambiguity attached to *his* in the term *his Maker*. If the antecedent of *his* is *he who oppresses*, then the proverb is telling us that an oppressor of the poor is reproaching his own maker; if the antecedent of *his* is *the poor*, then an oppressor of the poor man is reproaching the poor man's maker.

This kind of ambiguity appears frequently in Proverbs and begins to look suspiciously deliberate. If the ambiguity is deliberate, the point may well be that oppressing the poor reproaches God in two ways: it is a reproach to the Creator when his creation behaves unseemly, and it is a reproach to the Creator when his work is attacked or abused.

Asymmetrical Antithetical Parallelisms

The most transparent antithetical parallelisms are those which we have just examined, those which display a symmetry of both form and sense. All the meaning of such proverbs lies clearly exposed in the precisely paired contrasts of each idea. When this symmetry is disturbed in either form or sense, a more difficult proverb results. Such proverbs are called asymmetrical antithetical parallelisms. The difficulty of these proverbs, however, is also the source of their strength. The asymmetrical antithetical parallelism invites you to make various inferences from one idea to another in order to restore the symmetry which is lacking in the explicit words of the proverb. As you restore, to some degree, the balance which is lacking, meaning emerges from the proverb which was otherwise hidden.

A simple example of this kind of proverb is Proverbs 10:5, which is diagrammed below:

10:5a	10:5b
he who gathers	he who sleeps
in summer	in harvest
is	is
a son who	a son who
acts wisely	acts shamefully

The formal symmetry of this proverb is very precise. However, the sense of the various paired elements is asymmetrical. We apprehend almost immediately that Proverbs 10:5

is an antithetical parallelism, but some of the elements which are paired on opposing sides of the formal contrast are not really contrasts.

The subjects of each line do not contrast well on the surface; *gathering* is not the opposite of *sleeping*. However, the son who is sleeping is obviously not gathering during the harvest, and the son who gathers is evidently not asleep when he does so. Thus, even though there is some apparent asymmetry in the subjects, they are probably to be understood as loose contrasts.

The situation is different, however, in the last clause of each line. *Wisely* and *shamefully* are not contrasts at all. Throughout Proverbs the proper contrast with *wisdom* is *folly*, and the proper contrast with *shame* is *honor*. Though *wisely* and *shamefully* are paired formally in this proverb, their meanings have no explicit balancing contrast in the other line. To supply the balance of sense to Proverbs 10:5 we would need to make certain inferences. These inferences are based on contrasts which are implied but not stated:

10:5a	10:5b
he who gathers	he who sleeps
in summer	in harvest
is	is
a son who	a son who
acts wisely	(acts foolishly)
(acts honorably)	acts shamefully

The inferences are placed in parentheses in the diagram to distinguish them from the explicit statements of the proverb. When the sense of Proverbs 10:5 is fleshed out in this manner, still more lessons are suggested.

If gathering in summer is wise, then Proverbs 10:5 implies that sleeping in the time of harvest is folly. There is time enough to sleep when the conditions are not good for harvest, as in the autumn when the rains make harvesting an impossibility. Anyone who sleeps away the only opportunity to harvest the crops is a fool. On the other hand, there is more at stake than just the character of the worker; his actions also reflect upon the reputation of his parents. A son who acts wisely brings honor to the parents who reared him; conversely, the son who acts foolishly brings shame to his parents, who must claim a son who sleeps when he should be gathering.

Proverbs 11:1 is another antithetical parallelism with precise formal symmetry but some asymmetry in the sense of two elements which are paired:

11:1a	**11:1b**
a false balance	a just weight
is	is
to the LORD	His
an abomination	delight

In making this diagram, the word order is altered in order to pair the corresponding elements from each line with one another. The words *abomination* and *delight* are good contrasts. However, *false* and *just* are not contrasts; *true* is the proper contrast of *false*, and *unjust* is the proper contrast of *just*.

A diagram of Proverbs 11:1 with these contrasts supplied in their appropriate places would look like this:

11:1a	**11:1b**
a false	a (true)
(unjust)	just
balance	weight
is	is
to the LORD	His
an abomination	delight

41

When both the explicit and implicit ideas of this proverb are seen, they provide a needed corrective to modern American notions of justice. Modern conceptions of justice are apt to revolve around notions of legal courts or legislatures which mandate justice through statute. On the other hand, injustice is mostly thought of as a violation of rights which a government grants to its citizens. Proverbs 11:1 makes justice a crucial commodity of the marketplace, an issue between a buyer and a seller. Furthermore, God himself stands behind this union of truth and justice in business dealings. True balances and just weights delight the God of all justice; he whose name is Truth regards the false and the unjust as abominable. Service to such a God does not end in the Temple or the church meeting. It extends to the market, trading floor, showroom and board meeting.

In the previous examples, the proverbs displayed symmetry in form, and both symmetry and asymmetry in content. In Proverbs 10:5 and 11:1, the asymmetry arose from elements which were formally paired but were not precise contrasts. Proverbs contains many examples in which there is still symmetry of form but complete asymmetry in sense.

One example of this kind of proverb is 28:27:

28:27a	**28:27b**
he who gives	he who shuts
to the poor	his eyes
will never want	will have many curses

As it stands, there is a formal symmetry in the way the ideas of 28:27 are composed and paired; the subjects are formed in the same pattern, and each predicate expresses a consequence of the activity in the subject. However, the phrase *who gives to the poor* does not properly contrast with *who shuts his eyes;* similarly, the phrase *will never want* is not really the antithesis of *will have many curses.* Nevertheless, Proverbs 28:27 clearly displays antithetical parallelism, although precise contrasts are not expressed anywhere in the proverb.

When all the suppressed contrasts are exposed, several interesting traits of each character appear.

28:27a	28:27b
he who gives to	(he who withholds from
the poor	the poor)
(he who opens his eyes)	he who shuts his eyes
will never want	(will want)
(will have many blessings)	will have many curses

We discover that the one who is giving to the poor does so because he is alert to those in need, and as he finds them he helps them. On the other hand, the person who is withholding from the poor does so through willful ignorance of their plight. He refuses to look at them and so does not fill their needs. The alert giver will never lack anything, and the contrast suggests why this is so. He will reap many blessings which will supply his lack even as he has supplied the lack of others. The one who shuts his eyes and his hand will have many curses. Again, the contrast in this proverb indicates that this will result in his having want himself.

All these ideas are expressed in other parts of Solomon's proverbs (compare 17:5; 19:17; 21:13; 22:22-23). The asymmetry of Proverbs 28:27 permits many ideas to be compressed into few words. As you expose through inference what is latent in the proverb, the message of the proverb expands in surprising and unexpected ways.

Proverbs 28:27 is also a good example of the kind of problem which can arise as you attempt to balance the asymmetry of a proverb through inference. Consider, for example, the subject of 28:27a: "he who gives to the poor." Which idea shall we infer as the most proper contrast for 28:27b—he who does not *give* to the poor or he who *withholds* from the poor?

Certainly, it would be safe and accurate to infer the former. However, in 28:27b we find a fellow who shuts his eyes, presumably a deliberate and purposeful activity. In the context of this proverb, such shutting of the eyes must be solely to avoid beholding the plight of the poor. Therefore, we conclude that the person who is shutting his eyes is not merely failing to give to the poor, he is actively withholding aid from them.

A similar problem arises in contrasting the predicates of 28:27. The stingy man is said to *have many curses*. Does this imply that the generous man will simply lack curses, or will he also have many blessings? It is hard to imagine that the mere lack of curses will result in lack of poverty, especially as the person who is giving to the poor is depleting his own resources to do so. If he is to escape poverty himself as a result of his own generosity, his resources must be replenished and enriched. From other proverbs it is clear that God is the one who enriches and restores what the generous person gives away (see Prov 19:17). Several hundred years after Solomon collected this proverb, we find Paul encouraging the Corinthian church that God still supplies the resources for a ministry of giving (2 Cor 9:10-11).

In all the previous examples the asymmetry in sense has been easy to recognize because the proverbs were symmetrical in form. When a proverb exhibits formal symmetry, it is easy to pair up the formal elements and then decide whether or not they constitute good contrasts with one another. When asymmetry in sense is discerned, then you can make whatever inferences are required to balance the sense of the proverb. This procedure becomes almost mechanical for proverbs which display formal symmetry. However, the process of inferring suppressed contrasts becomes more difficult as the asymmetry of the proverb's form increases.

Consider, for example, Proverbs 14:16: "A wise man is cautious and turns away from evil,/But a fool is arrogant and careless." Although this proverb is asymmetrical in form, it may be diagrammed in such a way as to expose the suppressed contrasts.

14:16a	14:16b
a wise man	a fool
is	is
cautious	careless
(and humble)	and arrogant
and turns away from evil	(does not turn away from evil)

Because of the obvious antithetical parallelism, it is not difficult to make the inferences which appear in the parentheses above. In this proverb, the inferences restore not only a balance of sense, but something of a balance in form as well.

Sometimes simple paraphrasing will transform formal asymmetry into formal symmetry so that easy diagramming is possible. Proverbs 11:6, for example, has verbs in different voices: "The righteousness of the upright will deliver them,/ But the treacherous will be caught by their own greed." The verb in the first line is in the active voice, while the verb in the second line is in the passive voice. For this reason, it is impossible to pair formally the genuinely contrasting elements of this proverb in a diagram, for they appear in differing syntactical relationships in their own sentences.

If, however, the voice of either verb is altered to conform to the voice of the other verb and the necessary paraphrasing is done to maintain the sense, then the following diagram may be made:

11:6a	11:6b
(the generosity)	the greed
the righteousness	(the unrighteousness)
of the upright	of the treacherous
will deliver them	will capture them

In the diagram above the second line of 11:6 was rewritten in the active voice. If instead the first line is rewritten in the passive voice, the following diagram results:

11:6a	11:6b
the upright	the treacherous
will be delivered	will be captured
by their righteousness	(by their unrighteousness)
(by their generosity)	by their greed

Either way *upright* and *treacherous* are clear contrasts, as are the verbs *deliver* and *capture*. *Righteousness* and *greed*, however, are not good contrasts, even though we would understand greed to be a form of unrighteousness. Yet because of this contrast, we infer that the righteousness which the proverb has in mind is generosity. This same expressing of righteousness through generosity lies behind the preaching of John the Baptist. When the multitudes asked him what works he was speaking of which were befitting the repentance he demanded, John answered, "He who has two coats, let him share with him who has none; and he who has food, let him do likewise" (Lk 3:10-11 RSV). He further admonished the tax gatherers not to collect more than what was due, and the soldiers were exhorted to be satisfied with their wages and to avoid using their power to extort money (Lk 3:12-14). In John's day as well as in Solomon's, the righteous generosity of the upright would deliver them. The treacherous, who would profess repentance without any change of behavior, would be caught in their own greed.

Some proverbs are so asymmetrical in form that they cannot be easily rewritten. Others can still be diagrammed. Proverbs 11:2, for example, has no formal symmetry at all: "When pride comes, then comes dishonor,/But with the humble is wisdom." A diagram of this proverb, which exposes a suppressed contrast, looks like this:

11:2a	**11:2b**
when pride comes	with the humble
	is
(folly)	wisdom
then comes dishonor	(honor)

In this diagram the phrase *with the humble* is paired with *when pride comes* because they are contrasts in sense. *Dishonor* and *wisdom* are not contrasts, so their contrasts are supplied in parentheses.

What this diagram exposes is the source of the dishonor for the proud person. Pride moves a person to behave foolishly so that he is dishonored. The genuinely humble person might be completely overlooked, except for the wisdom which comes with humility. Because of skill in living, the humble person attracts the honor of those who see his success. In a similar way, the folly which the proud person commits draws attention, though not the attention of esteem, but rather shame.

Some proverbs are so asymmetrical in form that no diagramming is possible. One such proverb is 12:15: "The way of a fool is right in his own eyes,/But a wise man is he who listens to counsel." All efforts to paraphrase either side of the proverb in order to bring it into sufficient formal symmetry produces an extremely cumbersome result hardly worth the effort. Nevertheless, it is clear that a contrast is being made, even though it is suppressed.

The unraveling of this proverb commences when we merely infer the contrast of either line relative to its partner. If the wise man listens to counsel, then the fool does not. Therefore, the complete message of 12:15 concerning the fool is that he does not listen to counsel (implicit), and that his way is right in his own eyes (explicit). What is implied about the fool becomes the consequence of what is explicitly said about him. As the fool's way is right in his own eyes, he not only refuses to listen to counsel, he probably rejects whatever is offered to him (compare Prov 1:7). On the other hand, if the fool's way is right in his own eyes, it is implied that the wise man's way is not right in his own eyes. The wise man does not trust his own perception of matters, but seeks out the viewpoints of others. He does not lean on his own understanding. What is implied about the wise man in 12:15 becomes the explanation for what is explicitly said about him.

Beginners' Blunders and Bungles
Before they ever learn to ride a bicycle themselves, little boys and girls see their friends cruising effortlessly. It looks so easy to ride on two wheels, or even one wheel if their older friends can do wheelies. When the bicycle arrives on Christmas morning or during a birthday celebration, hopes are fulfilled; when the first few rides are attempted, hopes are dashed. What looked so easy is found to be very hard.

Something very like this child's disappointment often settles over students as they begin to gambol through Solomon's proverbs, applying some simple technique or concept which unlocks some of their tightly held wisdom. Some of the proverbs, for example, are easily seen to be antithetical or synonymous parallelisms. Some of the antithetical parallelisms are easily seen to be symmetrical or asymmetrical. Some of the asymmetrical proverbs are easily balanced through simple inferences. But sooner or later—usually sooner—the eager student of wisdom finds a proverb which is not so easy. Then he or she happens upon some which are not easy at all or discovers those that are positively difficult. When the apparently simple procedure of diagramming asymmetrical parallelisms is attempted in order to balance the asymmetry, the results are either trivial or nonsensical. Disappointment and frustration rear their ugly heads.

The beginner has two problems: a misunderstanding of the method used in studying the proverbs, and a lack of experience in applying that method. The following warnings will help you to avoid these pitfalls.

Warning Number One: Each word on one side of an antithetical parallelism does not need to have a contrast on the other side of the parallelism. This is clear from those perfectly symmetrical antithetical parallelisms we examined early in this chapter. Consider again the diagram of Proverbs 10:1:

10:1a	10:1b
a wise son	a foolish son
makes	is
a glad	a grief
father	mother

Note the contrast between the subjects of each line: the contrast with *a wise son* is *a foolish son*, not something like *a foolish daughter* or *a foolish non-son*. On the other hand, *father* and *mother* are not intended to be contrasts in this proverb, but rather stylistic variants for *parents*.

You may sometimes misapply the relationship of contrast in an asymmetrical parallelism, thinking that each element on any side of the parallelism must find a contrast on the other side. A misguided student might take Proverbs 14:21, "He who despises his neighbor sins,/But happy is he who is gracious to the poor," and diagram it like this:

14:21a	14:21b
he who despises	he who is gracious
his (rich) neighbor	to the poor (stranger)
sins	(does righteousness)
(is unhappy)	is happy

This diagram goes astray in pairing *neighbor* and *poor*. Because the student misunderstood these terms to require contrasting elements, he provided *rich neighbor* to contrast with *poor stranger,* an odd contrast indeed. Actually, *neighbor* and *the poor* are synonymous elements in an antithetical parallelism. Proverbs 14:21 is speaking about behavior directed at *the poor* who are our *neighbors,* the poor in our midst.

Beginning students often have a misunderstanding about antithetical parallelisms. They suppose that every word in each line must have a contrast in the corresponding line. This almost never happens. In fact, antithetical parallelisms often contain elements which are synonymous or even identical. For example, a wise *son* is contrasted with a foolish *son,* or a sluggard's *work* with the *work* of a diligent man.

These examples also illustrate that proverbs tend to contrast wisdom and folly concretely rather than abstractly. People are wise or foolish in child raising, money management, personal relationships, their relationship to God, or dozens of other areas of living to which the proverbs speak.

Warning Number Two: When in doubt about what contrast to supply in balancing an asymmetrical parallelism, merely supply the negation of the element you are trying to balance. Searching for nonexistent antonyms is a waste of time.

For example, consider Proverbs 17:9: "He who covers a transgression seeks love,/But he who repeats a matter separates intimate friends." Against the background of interpersonal relationships, the phrase *seeks love* is perhaps a sufficient contrast with *separates intimate friends.* However, the words *repeats a matter* do not form a good contrast with *covers a transgression.* Proverbs 17:9, therefore, is making a suppressed contrast which is exposed in the diagram below:

17:9a	17:9b
he who covers	(he who does not cover
a transgression	a transgression)
(he who does not repeat	he who repeats
a matter)	a matter
seeks love	separates intimate friends

In making the inferences for this diagram, it is sufficient to infer that *he who does not cover* is a contrast for *he who covers.* Similarly, *he who repeats a matter* is sufficiently contrasted with *he who does not repeat a matter.* Indeed, by inferring these simple negations in order to balance the contrasts of each line, we learn what covering a transgression looks like in practice: merely refusing to repeat something which one has seen or heard is all that is required.

Warning Number Three: Beware of figures of speech, as these pose special problems in making inferences. Consider, for example, Proverbs 27:6: "Faithful are the wounds of a friend,/But deceitful are the kisses of an enemy." *Wounds* and *kisses* might be some sort of contrast, as they are opposite kinds of physical contact between persons. However, in this proverb friends are making wounds and enemies are giving kisses. Surely something other than concrete kisses and wounds are being considered here. How is it that faithfulness can be a property of a wound or deceitfulness a characteristic of kisses? The answer lies in the figurative use of the words in Proverbs 27:6. Figures of speech and their proper interpretation must be taken into account in order to discern the parallelism of a proverb and to make any inferences necessary to balance its asymmetry. Until you become comfortable with the matters discussed in chapters seven through ten of this book, you should defer applying the study techniques discussed in this chapter.

Warning Number Four: Do not become disillusioned if every proverb in Solomon's collection does not become transparent. Remember that wisdom comes by doing, not by reading a book. Some of the proverbs are simple, and they are designed for the simple, those who are just beginning to exercise their spirits to know wisdom. As skill is acquired through practice, more and more proverbs will begin to open up like rosebuds. "Knowledge is easy to him who has understanding," Solomon says in Proverbs 14:6. The beginner does not have the understanding to fathom more than a portion of the simpler proverbs.

Even those who are wise will not exhaust the proverbs of Solomon, though they can always hear and gain more wisdom. At the end of his life, Solomon himself confessed that his determination to be wise had ended in failure: "I said, 'I will be wise,' but it was far from me. What has been is remote and exceedingly mysterious. Who can discover it?" (Eccles 7:23-24). Nevertheless, this was the same Solomon who praised wisdom repeatedly in Proverbs 1—9 and who was responsible for composing and collecting the wisdom contained in the rest of Proverbs. If we may never be wise, at least we can always be wiser. Faithful attention to Solomon's proverbs may never deliver us at a destination, but it will keep us walking in the path.

Study Questions: Chapter Four
1. Read carefully the following proverbs and determine for each whether it is symmetrical or asymmetrical in *sense*. Many of them will be symmetrical in form, yet asymmetrical in sense.

☐ The wages of the righteous is life,
The income of the wicked, punishment. (10:16)
☐ The integrity of the upright will guide them,
But the falseness of the treacherous will destroy them. (11:3)
☐ He who is surety for a stranger will surely suffer for it,
But he who hates going surety is safe. (11:15)
☐ The merciful man does himself good,
But the cruel man does himself harm. (11:17)
☐ The perverse in heart are an abomination to the LORD,
But the blameless in their walk are His delight. (11:20)
☐ The one who guards his mouth preserves his life;
The one who opens wide his lips comes to ruin. (13:3)
☐ There is one who pretends to be rich, but has nothing;
Another pretends to be poor, but has great wealth. (13:7)
☐ He who walks in his uprightness fears the LORD,
But he who is crooked in his ways despises Him. (14:2)
☐ A faithful witness will not lie,
But a false witness speaks lies. (14:5)
☐ The house of the wicked will be destroyed,
But the tent of the upright will flourish. (14:11)
☐ A truthful witness saves lives,
But he who speaks lies is treacherous. (14:25)
☐ Righteousness exalts a nation,
But sin is a disgrace to any people. (14:34)
☐ The poor man utters supplications,
But the rich man answers roughly. (18:23)
☐ The execution of justice is joy for the righteous,
But is terror to the workers of iniquity. (21:15)
☐ Those who forsake the law praise the wicked,

But those who keep the law strive with them. (28:5)

2. Diagram those proverbs which you have identified as asymmetrical in sense in the way such proverbs were diagrammed in chapter four, supplying in parentheses whatever is required to balance the sense of the proverb.

[CHAPTER FIVE]

Cerebral Cartooning: Emblematic Parallelisms

THERE ARE SEVEN OR EIGHT references to weather in the book of Proverbs. Proverbs 30:4 mentions the wind, while 25:23 speaks of the north wind and 10:25 talks about the whirlwind. Clouds and wind together are mentioned in Proverbs 25:14. We find references to steady rain (27:15), driving rain (28:3), rain and snow (26:1), and early chill (25:13). Nevertheless, Proverbs is a book of wisdom, not a Mideastern meteorological manual.

All these references to weather arise in Proverbs as examples, types, patterns or emblems of some intangible idea or experience. We are told in 1 Kings 4:33 that Solomon was a student of botany and biology: "He spoke of trees, from the cedar that is in Lebanon even to the hyssop that grows on the wall; he spoke also of animals and birds and creeping things and fish." It is not strange, therefore, to find in Solomon's collection of wisdom many proverbs which take the form of object lessons drawn from nature.

Of all the flora and fauna mentioned in 1 Kings 4:33, only fish are not mentioned in the book of Proverbs. We find proverbs built around animals such as badgers (30:26), donkeys (26:3), bears (17:12), lions (19:12), swine (11:22), oxen (14:4), dogs (26:11), goats (27:27), horses (21:31), lizards (30:28), serpents (30:19) and vipers (23:32). We may learn wisdom from the ant (30:25), locust (30:27) and leech (30:15). Although bees are not mentioned, the honeycomb is (16:24). Birds are mentioned generally (27:8) as well as specifically in the cock (30:31), raven (30:17), sparrows and swallows (26:2), and the eagle (30:19). Among plants we read of apples (25:11), grass (19:12), vines (24:30), leaves (11:28), roots (12:3), nettles (27:31), thorns (15:19), grain (27:22) and fig trees (27:18).

Solomon's breadth of knowledge in natural science coupled with his skill in casting proverbs into parallelisms naturally led to his collecting proverbs which compare some natural object or process with an intangible wisdom principle. One class of parallelism is distinguishable solely by its purpose to illustrate an intangible truth by some concrete emblem.

Emblematic Parallelisms

A proverb exhibits emblematic parallelism when the first line is an emblem, illustration, type or example drawn from nature or daily life. The concrete emblem in the first line serves to express in tangible form the wisdom principle of the second line. The two lines are to be compared. Often there is a riddle posed in this kind of parallelism, and in such cases you must ferret out the particulars of the comparison.

The comparison in an emblematic parallelism is not difficult to perceive. Sometimes it is announced explicitly as in Proverbs 27:15:

A constant dripping on a day of steady rain

And a contentious woman are alike.
In other proverbs the emblem in the first line is simply equated with the subject of the second line, though often the English versions will supply the word *like* at the beginning of the first line. Proverbs 25:18 and 19 are examples:
Like a club and a sword and a sharp arrow
Is a man who bears false witness against his neighbor.
Like a bad tooth and an unsteady foot
Is confidence in a faithless man in time of trouble.
In other proverbs the coordinating conjunctions *like* and *so* announce the comparison, as in Proverbs 10:26:
Like vinegar to the teeth and smoke to the eyes,
So is the lazy one to those who send him.
At other times the two lines will be simply connected by the lexically versatile *we*, which often appears in English versions as "and," as in Proverbs 25:23:
The north wind brings forth rain,
And a backbiting tongue, an angry countenance.
There are even a few emblematic parallelisms in which the Hebrew has no conjunction at all, but merely juxtaposes the two lines. The conjunctions are often supplied in the English translation. Consider Proverbs 11:22 and 25:27:

As a ring of gold in a swine's snout,
So is a beautiful woman with no taste. (my translation)

It is not good to eat much honey,
Nor is it glory to search out one's own glory.

In one sense, emblematic parallelisms function like synonymous parallelisms. However, the feature which distinguishes emblematic parallelisms as a separate class is the *emblem*—the concrete image or illustration, event or process, drawn from nature or human experience. In synonymous parallelisms the first line is repeated in the second line; in emblematic parallelisms the first line illustrates the second line.

Cerebral Cartooning

By its very design the emblematic parallelism invites comparison between the emblem and that thing for which the emblem stands. Emblematic parallelisms function very much like political cartoons in newspaper editorials. Often very abstract political affirmations are rendered intelligible by means of a concrete image in the cartoon coupled with a caption. In emblematic parallelisms, the first line serves as the picture, the second line as the caption. In meditating on an emblematic parallelism, the student seeks to discern the trait or traits which the picture and the caption have in common. In Proverbs 25:13, this commonality is made explicit:

Like the cold of snow in the time of harvest
Is a faithful messenger to those who send him,
For he refreshes the soul of his masters.

Just as the cold snow would refresh the hot, perspiring laborers during harvest time, so a faithful messenger refreshes his masters by dutifully accomplishing the mission on which they sent him. The point of comparing snowy cold and a faithful messenger is stated clearly in the proverb.

The very next proverb in the book, Proverbs 25:14, also makes a meteorological comparison, but the point of the comparison is not stated:

Like clouds and wind without rain
Is a man who boasts of his gifts falsely.

The point of this comparison is not so difficult to fathom. We need only imagine ourselves as a farmer with seed in the ground or tender plants barely sprouted in a semiarid farming area; clouds and wind without rain would prove a disappointment. So would a man who boasted of his gifts falsely. Such a man would raise hopes of profit and advantage in those to whom he boasted, yet such hopes would be dashed to the degree that the man's boasting was false.

The scope of the comparison between the two lines of an emblematic parallelism can vary significantly. In some proverbs the scope of the comparison is very narrow, as in Proverbs 25:13 where the man and snow are compared because they both bring refreshment. Another proverb with a seemingly narrow scope of comparison is Proverbs 27:17:

Iron sharpens iron,

So one man sharpens another.

The scope of the comparison is restricted to the sharpening. The lesson of this proverb is that each person changes in the process, not just one of them.

On the other hand, some proverbs invite you to discover seemingly unlimited similarities between the two things which are compared in the proverb. Proverbs 27:15 is such a proverb:

A constant dripping on a day of steady rain

And a contentious woman are alike.

The two things which are being compared are *dripping* and a *contentious woman*. There appear to be no limits set as you seek to specify the points of the comparison. Indeed, the amplification of *dripping* by the words *constant* and *on a day of steady rain* have the effect of encouraging you to expand your elaboration beyond the obvious point—both are irritations.

It is well within the boundaries of the comparison, for example, to see that the contentious woman's irritation is constant, even as the dripping is. Like a dripping on a day of steady rain, her irritation is in small increments which are nothing in themselves, but they have a cumulative effect which can be massive. Her irritations are something which no one can control, even as the rain cannot be stopped. Her "dripping" may cause various reactions in those around her —crankiness and irascibility, short attention span, low productivity and strong efforts to cover the distraction with other interests, much as one would turn on a bedroom fan to mask a dripping faucet. You can use every imaginable irritation caused by a dripping faucet to expand the comparison between dripping and a contentious woman.

Unraveling the Riddle

All emblematic parallelisms qualify as riddles. Behind every statement "A is like B" is the question *"how is A like B?"* Though we commonly speak in comparisons without posing countless riddles to those who hear us, Solomon's proverbs are not common speech. Every comparison which the proverbs make is an invitation to elaborate the particulars of the comparison. "How is A like B?" must be asked of every emblematic parallelism.

There are two steps in solving the puzzle which an emblematic parallelism poses. The first step is to find elements in the emblem which accurately correspond to elements in the caption of the proverb. Sometimes this is very easy, as in Proverbs 27:15, considered above. In that proverb *dripping* corresponds to a *contentious woman.*

However, many emblematic parallelisms will have several elements in each line which must be properly paired in order to solve the riddle. Proverbs 27:17, for example, has three elements in each line. In the emblem there are two pieces of iron and the sharpening process between the two. In the second line there are two men and a "sharpening" process between them. Obviously the two men are represented by the two pieces of iron, and the interaction between them corresponds to the sharpening of the one piece of iron by the other.

In the other proverbs, however, finding the corresponding elements is something of a puzzle in itself. For example, consider Proverbs 25:11:
Like apples of gold in settings of silver
Is a word spoken in right circumstances.
The element in the first line represents the work of a jeweler

or other craftsman who renders apples in gold in a background and framing of silver—possibly leaves or filigree. We may never have seen a particular work such as this, but a little imagination suffices to conjure up the image of an intricate, skillfully executed piece of jewelry. Beneath this image we may visualize the caption "A word spoken in right circumstances."

The picture and the caption can be paired in two ways. One possibility is to pair the entire piece of jewelry with the aptly spoken word. In this case the point of the proverb would be that such a word functions as a piece of finely wrought jewelry—it adorns, attracts attention to its obvious beauty, is memorable to its hearers. Another possibility, however, is to link the apples of gold with the word and the settings of silver with the right circumstances. The previous point would still be made, but the proverb would also express the idea that the jewel-like beauty of such a word arises not only from the way it is crafted, but also from the setting in which the word is spoken. There is more to excellent speech than a nicely turned phrase; it is also necessary that the word be spoken in apt circumstances. When both are present, a verbal jewel results.

Some emblematic parallelisms present several possibilities for correspondences. One of these is Proverbs 25:18:

Like a club and a sword and a sharp arrow
Is a man who bears false witness against his neighbor.

Though the caption of this proverb is wordier than the emblem, it sets forth only one element—a man who lies against his neighbor. The emblem, however, is triple—a club, a sword and a sharp arrow! We might suppose, at the beginning, that these three are mentioned in order to raise in our minds that class of things of which they are members—instruments of war. The point of the comparison then would be that bearing false witness against one's neighbor is tantamount to waging war against him. Specifying implements of warfare would heighten the sense of personal attack which the liar is directing at his neighbor.

Is there anything else indicated by this threefold emblem? Might a man who bears false witness against his neighbor be more like *one* of these implements than the others? From a club to a sharp arrow we move along a progression of increasing refinement in the weapon and also a progression toward decreasing personal contact with the one attacked. Bludgeoning someone to death is certainly a messier and more immediate proposition than killing him at long distance with a well-aimed arrow. The selection of weapons in the emblem and their ordering may be suggesting the range of ways in which lying can accomplish hostile intentions.

After the correspondences between the emblem and the caption have been made, the next step in solving the puzzle in an emblematic parallelism is to explicate all the details encompassed in the comparison. The discussions of the previous two proverbs indicate the way in which this step proceeds—from the obvious to the less obvious, from the simple to the subtle. Beyond this, nothing more may be said about unraveling the riddles of these proverbs. Their great profit consists in their capacity to be unraveled, to be explicated, to be meditated upon. As you exercise yourself in fathoming the depths of some comparison, you will gain more skill in the very process itself. You learn to walk by walking.

Where to Go for Weather Reports
Proverbs 25:23 appeals to the weather for wisdom:
    The north wind brings forth rain,
    And a backbiting tongue, an angry countenance.
In this emblematic parallelism the correspondences instruct us to expect an angry countenance to follow in the wake of a backbiting tongue every bit as much as rain follows in the wake of the north wind. It has been an embarrassment to commentators that in Palestine the north wind is dry and

never brings rain. Jerome, when he translated the Old Testament into Latin, knew the weather patterns of Palestine and rendered the proverb *ventus aquilo dissipat pluvias, et facies tristis linguam detrahentem*—"the north wind drives away rain, and an angry face a disparaging tongue," which translation is followed in the King James Version. Nevertheless, the Hebrew verb cannot mean "drives away." It is enough to suppose that the proverb originated somewhere other than Palestine and Solomon added it to his collection.

Indeed, most people who read Proverbs 25:23 can see the obvious lesson in it without ever knowing which wind brings forth rain, whether in Palestine or any other part of the world. It has been a common observation worldwide for thousands of years that rains come from the same direction with some degree of regularity. Therefore, when the wind blows from that point on the compass, we expect rain will follow in its wake.

Knowledge of nature therefore is not only helpful in understanding the emblematic proverbs, it is essential; for emblematic parallelisms are drawn largely from nature and common human experience. Where our experience and knowledge match that of the emblems in these proverbs, we can ponder them profitably. Where we lack experience or knowledge, the proverbs will remain opaque.

Proverbs 27:15, which was considered earlier, likely arose in times when roofs leaked easily or when the drainage around the outside of dwellings was not so modern or silent as it is today. We do not often complain about the sound of rain outside our houses. We do complain, however, of the sound of a dripping faucet. If our experience or knowledge does not precisely match that found in a proverb, we may have other experiences which are similar. From these we may meditate profitably without fear of being misled.

When our experience or the observation of others' experiences is lacking completely, imagination can often come to

our aid. Consider Proverbs 25:19, for example:
Like a bad tooth and an unsteady foot
Is confidence in a faithless man in time of trouble.
We may meditate profitably on this proverb even if we have never had a cavity in our life and our feet have always been steady. However, those with loose caps on their teeth or sprained ankles in the midst of a rush-hour crowd are far better equipped to ponder this proverb.

Some proverbs, however, will remain obscure to us unless and until we are instructed concerning the nature of the emblems. One example of this is Proverbs 28:15:
Like a roaring lion and a rushing bear
Is a wicked ruler over a poor people.
Most people who live in industrialized society have never seen a lion or a bear, except in a zoo. They would have little or no knowledge of the habits of these animals. What does the proverb indicate, for example, when it specifies a *roaring* lion or a *rushing* bear? Only those who have some knowledge of these animals will get the point of the proverb.

When studying the emblematic proverb you must be a student of God's creation as well. Unraveling the emblematic parallelisms can be as much an education in nature and human experience as it is an education in wisdom. Certainly, you should not fail to resort to the instruction, observations and experience of others in your efforts to understand the nature of the emblems which are set forth for you to consider.

Study Questions: Chapter Five

1. Draw the appropriate correspondences between the emblem and the caption in Proverbs 27:19:

As in water face reflects face,
So the heart of man reflects man.

It may prove helpful to make a simple line drawing of the emblem and then label the parts of the picture with the elements mentioned in the second line of the proverb. What answer does this proverb give to the old philosophical exhortation "Know thyself"?

2. Consider Proverbs 25:26, which has two emblems:

Like a trampled spring and a polluted well
Is a righteous man who gives way before the wicked.

How are the emblems the same? How do they differ? What do both emblems together indicate about the righteous man which would not be indicated if only one of the emblems had been used?

3. Compare the emblems in the following translation of Proverbs 25:20:

Like one who takes off a garment on a cold day, or like vinegar on soda,
Is he who sings songs to a troubled heart.

How are these emblems the same? How do they differ? Are their similarities or differences emphasized in this proverb?

4. Draw a picture of a pig with a pretty piece of jewelry in its nose. Under the picture write the caption "A beautiful woman with no taste" (Prov 11:22). What in the picture represents the beautiful woman? What represents the lack of taste?

[CHAPTER SIX]

Conundrums & Other Mind Benders: Synthetic Parallelisms

WHEN STUDENTS OF ANY BRANCH of human learning set themselves to cataloguing and organizing the stuff of their study, they commonly group them into classes of things which have some traits in common. Lexicographers, for example, group all the words of a language which start with the letter *A* together, those which start with the letter *B* into another group, and so on until dictionaries are formed. Cookbooks may have their contents arranged according to common ingredients (pumpkin dishes, egg dishes, chicken dishes), common food groups (vegetable recipes, meat recipes), common courses (appetizers, soups, salads, desserts) or some other criterion (low-calorie dishes, Christmas recipes, low-budget items). Thus far in the study of Solomon's proverbs, we have catalogued the parallelisms they display according to a common feature: the pair of ideas repeat one another (synonymous parallelisms), contrast with one another (antithetical parallelisms), or one line illustrates the other (emblematic parallelisms).

Occasionally some class of things will be distinguished not so much by a trait they all have in common, but by some trait which they do *not* have. In some biological discussions, animals will be referred to by the classes vertebrates and invertebrates—those with and without spinal cords. The study of chemistry may be broadly divided into organic and inorganic—the latter branch dealing largely with chemical compounds unrelated to those which arise from plant or animal sources. In a similar fashion, those who analyze and describe the parallelisms of Solomon's proverbs denote a fourth class—the synthetic parallelism—which has as its first characteristic that it is not a synonymous, antithetical or emblematic parallelism.

Yet this is not the end of the matter. Not only are the synthetic parallelisms unlike the other kinds of parallelisms, they are only irregularly like each other. The synthetic parallelisms are actually a broad class of several different subclasses, some of which have discernible features, while others are very difficult to recognize. If there is any feature which all synthetic parallelisms have in common, it is that they pose subtle problems of interpretation. You must not only attempt to fathom how the pair of ideas relate to one another, but also seek to validate that relationship from elements or inferences within the proverb itself. The synthetic parallelisms easiest to recognize are those which have formal characteristics which "announce" the relationship between the pair of ideas in the parallelism.

Formal Synthetic Parallelisms
Some synthetic parallelisms may be recognized by their forms alone. Among these are parallelisms which specify various classes, those which argue from lesser to greater and

vice versa, and those which express a priority between two ideas. In all these parallelisms there are linguistic conventions—forms of speech—which announce the nature of the parallelism. This is what led some students of the proverbs to name these parallelisms *formal* parallelisms. However, as only some of the synthetic parallelisms have specific forms, it is best to speak of formal synthetic parallelisms as a subset of synthetic parallelisms.

Classifying proverbs. The simplest synthetic parallelisms are those which are not really parallelisms at all. They consist of a single sentence with the verb *is* or *are*. Their only function seems to be to delimit a class or to equate one class with another class.

One example of this kind of synthetic parallelism is Proverbs 19:26:

He who assaults his father and drives his mother away
Is a shameful and disgraceful son.

The transparency of this statement makes it seem, at first glance, too obvious for words. The activity in the first half of the proverb probably has in view the ruthless withholding of support from parents when they are in their old age. Such behavior on the part of a person would certainly qualify him as a shameful and disgraceful son. However, it is unlikely that his shameful and disgraceful behavior failed to be noticed until it came time for him "to make some return to [his] parents" (1 Tim 5:4). Such character defects would have been obvious long before. Proverbs 19:26 warns parents of such a son that they cannot expect him to behave in any other way than to aggressively reject them when they need his support.

Proverbs 17:15 neatly equates two classes that are not immediately equal to one another:

He who justifies the wicked, and he who condemns the righteous,
Both of them alike are an abomination to the LORD.

The immediate effect of the second half of this proverb is to dispel the notion that Israel's God views one activity as worse than the other. But if in God's estimation both activities are equally deplorable, perhaps this may indicate that the two activities are really the same: to justify the wicked is tantamount to condemning the righteous, and vice versa.

Another proverb which defines classes and relates them to one another is Proverbs 17:6:

Grandchildren are the crown of old men,
And the glory of sons is their fathers.

A peculiar honor or prize accrues to old men in their grandchildren; and though sons cannot view their fathers as rewards, they can and do boast of their fathers in anticipation of the same glory becoming manifest in them.

Some single-sentence proverbs are not classifying proverbs but rather exhibit another kind of synthetic parallelism. Consider, for example, Proverbs 15:31:

He whose ear listens to the life-giving reproof
Will dwell among the wise.

This proverb speaks of two classes: those who listen to life-giving reproof and those who dwell among the wise. The two classes are even equated insofar as the first class is said to eventually join the second. However, the point of the proverb seems not so much to equate these two classes as to place one class of activity prior to the other, either temporally, logically or both. We can expose the point of this proverb by paraphrasing it as follows: "He who would come eventually to dwell among the wise should, in the present time, turn his ear to hear life-giving reproof."

Argument from lesser to greater. Proverbs that argue from lesser to greater are very easy to recognize, for they have the formula "how much more" in the second line. An example of this kind of synthetic parallelism is Proverbs 15:11:

Sheol and Abaddon lie open before the LORD,
How much more the hearts of men!

The phrase "how much more," which begins the second line,

indicates that this parallelism is arguing from lesser to greater. Another example is Proverbs 11:31:
If the righteous will be rewarded in the earth,
How much more the wicked and the sinner!
Occasionally, there is an argument from greater to lesser, as in Proverbs 19:10:
Luxury is not fitting for a fool;
Much less for a slave to rule over princes.
These proverbs can be extremely difficult to fathom, for while their affirmation is very clear, not all the justification for their affirmation is expressed. When there is an argument from lesser to greater, it is assumed that the lesser case and the greater case have some element in common which varies only in degree. If some consequence results from the lesser case, then it results even more in the greater case. The puzzle in proverbs which use this form is to determine what the two cases have in common and how they differ. For example, consider Proverbs 21:27:
The sacrifice of the wicked is an abomination,
How much more when he brings it with evil intent!
A sacrifice in Old Testament worship was a means of fellowship with God, either to restore that fellowship when it had been broken by some transgression or to indulge in fellowship with him in response to some blessing or occasion for worship. The sacrifice of the wicked spoken of in Proverbs 21:27 envisions an unrepentant sinner going through the motions of fellowship with God when such fellowship does not exist. The abomination arises, therefore, from the hypocrisy and lie which such a sacrifice entails. The second line, however, envisions such a sacrifice with the additional feature that it is intended to accomplish something wicked in itself, as in making a sacrifice to impress others with one's own piety. If a sinner who offers sacrifice is an abomination, how much more a sinner who sacrifices in order to sin! In a similar way, all proverbs of the form "how much more" require you

to answer the question, Why is it so much more?

Better this than that. Proverbs which take the form "better this than that" are very easy to recognize because of the formulary way they are expressed. Except for one or two complex proverbs of more than two lines, these proverbs begin their first lines with *better* and their second lines with *than.*

Proverbs which affirm one thing as better than another are both clear and ambiguous. Their affirmations are clear, but the reason for their affirmations is not always clear. Behind every "better this than that" statement lies the question, *Why is this better than that?* These proverbs not only guide the naive by expressing a priority between things of differing value, they also exercise the wise who ponder how and why these proverbs are true. Consider Proverbs 16:16:

How much better it is to get wisdom than gold!

And to get understanding is to be chosen above silver.

Strictly speaking, this proverb exhibits synonymous, not synthetic, parallelism. However, the synonymous parallelism reveals that the purpose of affirming wisdom to be better than gold is so that we will *choose* wisdom rather than gold when both are offered to us. Since understanding is to be chosen *above* silver, we should decline the opportunity to receive money whenever we may instead take an opportunity to gain wisdom.

Why this is true is not discussed in Proverbs 16:16. However, in many other places in Proverbs the reason for this priority is discussed. Solomon's praise of wisdom in Proverbs 3:13-17 is probably the best example:

How blessed is the man who finds wisdom,

And the man who gains understanding.

For its profit is better than the profit of silver,

And its gain than fine gold.

She is more precious than jewels;

And nothing you desire compares with her.

Long life is in her right hand;

In her left hand are riches and honor.
Her ways are pleasant ways,
And all her paths are peace.

When faced with a choice, we should choose wisdom above riches for the same reason we would choose the goose over her golden eggs.

Yet life is seldom so simple as to offer us merely two choices. The proverbs which express priorities reflect this lack of simplicity. Most of them present complex evaluations involving more than simple either-or choices. Consider, for example, Proverbs 21:19:

It is better to live in a desert land,
Than with a contentious and vexing woman.

The options presented in this proverb are living alone and living with a vexing and contentious woman. Proverbs 21:19 places the premium on solitude, even if it is desertlike in its loneliness. Proverbs 21:9, however, affirms a more complex kind of priority:

It is better to live in a corner of a roof,
Than in a house shared with a contentious woman.

Cramped quarters are to be preferred to the spaciousness of a house shared with a contentious woman. Evidently she is far more confining than a roof corner. Proverbs 21:9 therefore urges the choice of confining physical shelter over the roominess of a house, if one's spirit can have room by making this choice. Room for the spirit is more important than room for the body.

Similar thoughts are expressed in Proverbs 17:1:

Better is a dry morsel and quietness with it
Than a house full of feasting with strife.

Normally we prefer feasting to nibbling on a dry crust of bread. However, quietness of spirit is far more important than food for the belly. Consequently, the quiet crust is better than the furious feast. The effect of this proverb is to elevate spiritual concerns above merely material ones.

Other Synthetic Parallelisms

In the synthetic parallelisms discussed previously, the relationship between the two lines was made explicit by the form of the proverbs. In many other synthetic parallelisms the relationship between the two lines is not explicit at all. In such cases you will need to ponder how they might relate to one another. The lexically ambiguous *we*, which many times introduces the second line of synthetic parallelisms, can mean "so," "and," "therefore," "as," "so that," "for" and several other quasi-logical meanings. Often the chief puzzle for the original Hebrew readers of the proverbs was to determine how the two lines were related to one another. The ways in which nonformal synthetic parallelisms relate to one another fall into three groups.

Statement/consequence or application. In some synthetic parallelisms the first line makes a statement while the second line expresses some consequence of that statement or specifies some practical way to apply the proverb. Often the translators have made this relationship between the two lines explicit by supplying an inferential conjunction at the beginning of the second line. For example, consider Proverbs 20:4 and 20:19:

> The sluggard does not plow after the autumn,
> So he begs during harvest and has nothing.

> He who goes about as a slanderer reveals secrets,
> Therefore do not associate with a gossip.

Proverbs 20:4b specifies a consequence of the statement in 20:4a; Proverbs 20:19b is an application of the statement in 20:19a. Another proverb which indicates how it should be applied is Proverbs 17:14:

> The beginning of strife is like letting out water,
> So abandon the quarrel before it breaks out.

Sometimes the logical or temporal priority of the first line will be indicated by its beginning with the word *when*, as in Proverbs 16:7:

When a man's ways are pleasing to the LORD,
He makes even his enemies to be at peace with him.

Because a translator must sometimes make an interpretive judgment about the kind of parallelism which a proverb displays, it is a good practice for you to maintain some minimal skepticism concerning the "announced" kind of parallelism of the English versions. In chapter three Proverbs 13:19 was presented as an example of a proverb translated as if it were an antithetical parallelism, when actually it is a synthetic parallelism. The first line makes a statement: "Desire realized is sweet to the soul." The second line in the Hebrew text begins with *we*. The King James Version, Revised Standard Version and New American Standard Bible all translate it as "but"; the English version published by the Jewish Publication Society renders the word "and." Neither translation is correct. Desire realized is sweet to the soul whether the desire is righteous or wicked. *So* it is an abomination for fools to depart from evil. The second line of Proverbs 13:19 is drawing a consequence in the case of the fool for the truth expressed in the first line of the proverb.

The most challenging synthetic parallelisms are those which juxtapose two statements either with no conjunction at all or (in the English versions) with the word *and*. An example of the former is Proverbs 15:12:

A scoffer does not love one who reproves him,
He will not go to the wise.

The second line of 15:12 draws out a consequence of the first line. A wise man is one who would, in love, reprove a fool for his folly. Scoffers hate such reproof; therefore they avoid those who would give it. Proverbs 10:22 in the English versions begins its second line with *and:*

It is the blessing of the LORD that makes rich,

And He adds no sorrow to it.

Both lines can be understood coordinately, but a better sense is expressed if one line is subordinated to the other: "When the blessing of the LORD makes rich,/He adds no sorrow to it." In other words, one of the hallmarks of riches which the Lord's blessing brings is the freedom from all sorrow.

A few synthetic parallelisms take the form of a single sentence in which the subject is some activity and the consequence of the activity is expressed in the predicate of the sentence. An example of this kind of statement/consequence parallelism is Proverbs 15:31:

He whose ear listens to the life-giving reproof
Will dwell among the wise.

Statement/basis. Other synthetic parallelisms function in a manner exactly opposite to statement/consequence variety. In the statement/basis parallelism the first line makes a statement, and the second line provides the basis upon which the first statement can be made. The second line in some way validates the first line. In English versions some statement/basis parallelisms can be recognized by the conjunction *for* which introduces the second line of the proverb, as in Proverbs 16:26:

A worker's appetite works for him,
For his hunger urges him on.

Proverbs 16:10 and 16:12 demonstrate the way in which statement/consequence or application proverbs become statement/basis proverbs by rearranging the order of the lines in the parallelism. Proverbs 16:10 reads:

A divine decision is in the lips of the king;
His mouth should not err in judgment.

The second line of 16:10 is making an application of the statement in the first line. Proverbs 16:12 reverses these ideas:

It is an abomination for kings to commit wickedness,
For a throne is established on righteousness.

In this proverb the second line states the basis for the idea which is expressed in the first line.

Proverbs 15:12 was previously cited as an example of a statement/consequence-application proverb:

A scoffer does not love one who reproves him,

He will not go to the wise.

Proverbs 23:9 expresses something of the same idea but reverses the relationship in the parallelism:

Do not speak in the hearing of a fool,

For he will despise the wisdom of your words.

It is not unusual, in proverbs whose first lines are commandments or prohibitions, to find that the second line gives a reason for the exhortation.

Statement/purpose or result. A third class of synthetic parallelisms which poses peculiar problems in interpretation is that in which the second line expresses either a purpose or a result of the first line. Proverbs 17:23 is a good example of a parallelism in which the second line expresses the *purpose* of the first line:

A wicked man receives a bribe from the bosom

To pervert the ways of justice.

Of course, when a wicked man receives a bribe, justice becomes perverted; and so it could be argued that 17:23b is expressing the result of 17:23a. While this understanding would be true as far as it goes, it misses the point that in most cases of bribery, justice—if followed—would normally frustrate the goals of the wicked man. The giving and receiving of bribes are expressly done for the *purpose* of circumventing the normal course of the law.

Proverbs 15:24, on the other hand, mentions an activity and its *result:*

The path of life leads upward for the wise,

That he may keep away from Sheol below.

The way in which the wise man is spoken of in 15:24a indicates that he is already on the path; the result is that he is not on another path—the one that leads to the grave.

At times it is difficult to determine whether the second line of the proverb is expressing purpose or result. Consider, for example, Proverbs 14:27:

The fear of the LORD is a fountain of life,
That one may avoid the snares of death.

The first line of this proverb does not denote an activity, but rather states a fact. Does then the fear of the Lord result in avoiding the snares of death? Or does this proverb recommend that its readers fear the Lord so that they may avoid the snares of death? Either sense is possible, and there is no reason to suppose that both senses are not present in the proverb as it is written. You will find such ambiguities sufficiently often to arouse your suspicion that they are deliberate.

The question may arise as to how statement/purpose proverbs differ from statement/basis proverbs. Similarly, what is the difference between statement/result proverbs and statement/consequence proverbs? In one sense there is no difference: a consequence of some activity is also a result. However, in those proverbs which are classified as statement/ purpose or result, the element of intentionality is much stronger than in the other proverbs. Many times it will be very difficult to be dogmatic on the kind of parallelism which these proverbs display. You will profit by pondering which classification is *best* suited for any particular proverb. Perhaps these synthetic parallelisms most clearly illustrate that the process of meditation is every bit as important as the results.

Study Questions: Chapter Six

1. Which of the following proverbs are *classifying proverbs* as described in this chapter? Explain why those proverbs which are not classifying proverbs fail to fit this category of parallelism.

☐ He who returns evil for good,
Evil will not depart from his house. (17:13)

☐ He also who is slack in his work
Is brother to him who destroys. (18:9)

☐ Haughty eyes and a proud heart,
The lamp of the wicked, is sin. (21:4)

☐ He who shuts his ear to the cry of the poor
Will also cry himself and not be answered. (21:13)

☐ He who robs his father or his mother,
And says, "It is not a transgression,"
Is the companion of a man who destroys. (28:24)

2. Explain why the following proverb is true:
All the brothers of a poor man hate him;
How much more do his friends go far from him! (19:7)

3. Explain why the following proverbs are true:

☐ Let a man meet a bear robbed of her cubs,
Rather than a fool in his folly. (17:12)

☐ Better is open rebuke
Than love that is concealed. (27:5)

4. Identify the parallelism of the following proverbs as either statement/consequence or statement/basis:

☐ In the fear of the LORD there is strong confidence,
And his children will have refuge. (14:26)

☐ Everyone who is proud in heart is an abomination to the LORD;
Assuredly, he will not be unpunished. (16:5)

☐ Do not boast about tomorrow,
For you do not know what a day may bring forth. (27:1)

☐ He who turns away his ear from listening to the law,
Even his prayer is an abomination. (28:9)

□ To show partiality is not good,
  Because for a piece of bread a man will transgress. (28:21)
□ A man with an evil eye hastens after wealth,
  And does not know that want will come upon him. (28:22)
5. Identify the following proverbs as statement/purpose, statement/result, or as fitting either category:
□ The teaching of the wise is a fountain of life,
  To turn aside from the snares of death. (13:14)
□ A rebellious man seeks only evil,
  So a cruel messenger will be sent against him. (17:11)
□ Listen to counsel and accept discipline,
  That you may be wise the rest of your days. (19:20)
□ Be wise, my son, and make my heart glad,
  That I may reply to him who reproaches me. (27:11)

CHAPTER SEVEN

As Plain as the Nose on Your Face: Recognizing Figures of Speech

MATTHEW RECORDS A TIME when Jesus and the disciples entered a boat after a confrontation with the Pharisees and the Sadducees. In their haste to leave, the disciples forgot to take provisions with them (Mt 16:5). Jesus warned them, "Watch out and beware of the leaven of the Pharisees and Sadducees." Perplexed at what he meant by this admonition, they fastened on the absence of bread in an attempt to understand what Jesus had just said. "Perhaps he wants us to avoid purchasing bread from such men as we have just left on the shore," they may have thought. Jesus' exasperation is not difficult to perceive in his response to their discussion of his meaning:

"You men of little faith, why do you discuss among yourselves that you have no bread? Do you not yet understand or remember the five loaves of the five thousand, and how many baskets you took up? Or the seven loaves of the four thousand, and how many large baskets you took up? How is it that you do not understand that I did not speak to you concerning bread? But beware of the leaven of the Pharisees and the Sadducees." Then they understood that He did not say to beware of the leaven of bread, but of the teaching of the Pharisees and Sadducees. (Mt 16:8-12)

At another time Jesus lost most of his disciples when they failed to understand his teaching. Speaking in the synagogue in Capernaum, Jesus said:

He who eats My flesh and drinks My blood has eternal life; and I will raise him up on the last day. For My flesh is true food and My blood is true drink. He who eats My flesh and drinks My blood abides in Me, and I in him. As the living Father sent Me, and I live because of the Father, so he who eats Me, he also shall live because of Me. This is the bread which came down out of heaven; not as the fathers ate, and died, he who eats this bread shall live forever. (Jn 6:54-58)

John then records that many of Jesus' disciples grumbled, "This is a difficult statement; who can listen to it?" In both of these cases of misunderstanding, Jesus was employing figures of speech. The misunderstanding arose because Jesus' hearers did not recognize his remarks as figurative.

What Is Figurative and What Is Not

Defining figurative speech and distinguishing it from literal speech is sometimes a difficult matter. Hermeneutical manuals and even dictionaries will often define figurative and literal speech as the negations of each other: figurative speech is nonliteral and literal speech is nonfigurative. Literal speech will sometimes be spoken of as normal, obvious, usual, natural or proper; figurative speech, on the other hand, would be an abnormal, unusual, extravagant or exaggerated use of words.

Such attempts to distinguish literal and figurative speech

do not help very much, for the usual and customary sense of words is often a figurative one, and some figures of speech are so matter-of-fact that they fail to be recognized as figures by those who hear them (see Jn 6:35!). For example, a *bear*, in its literal sense, is a large, hairy animal; a *bear* on Wall Street, however, is a person who sells securities or commodities in expectation of a price decline. There are also *bulls* on Wall Street from time to time, but they are not the kind of bulls one would slaughter and turn into hamburger. Those who advocate a strong national military policy and the use of military force in international diplomacy are often referred to as *hawks*; those who favor international military disarmament are called *doves*. A malicious woman is a *cat*; her surly husband is a *cur*; their great-uncle Melvin Nurddingy is a *turkey*. For many people, animal names are used far more often in a figurative sense than in a literal one.

Most people are so accustomed to hearing and using figures of speech that they almost never consciously recognize them. Consider the following fictional account of an ignored wife's revenge on her husband:

John sat at the breakfast table, buried deeply in the morning newspaper. Occasional grunts and mutterings informed Mary that her husband was still alive behind the wall of newsprint. She noticed the teakettle was boiling and removed it from the stove. While she wondered how she might liberate her husband from the *City News*, an idea slowly dawned. Boiling water in hand, she approached her husband as carefully as if she were walking on eggs. The spout of the teakettle took careful aim between the lower edge of the paper and the edge of the table, beyond which lay the peaceful and unsuspecting territory of John's lap. "It's about time city hall woke up" were the last words John spoke before coming fully and warmly awake himself.

Every sentence in this episode contains at least one figure of speech; several sentences contain two or more. Nevertheless, the text which describes this little domestic drama is far from being lurid with figurative language. While many figures are used in this text, they are comfortable in their context and do not draw attention to themselves. It is normal, usual, natural and proper to use figures of speech. Therefore, these characteristics are useless in distinguishing literal from figurative uses of words.

There are, however, two criteria by which you may distinguish between figurative and literal uses of words. The first of these is concreteness. Some nouns are concrete rather than abstract. A poem is concrete; poetry is abstract. In general, concrete nouns are tangible—they have determinate boundaries in space and time; they have various physical properties which they display to human senses. Figures of speech arise when concrete words are employed in ways other than their primary concrete meaning. This suggests the second criterion for distinguishing figurative speech: when an attempt to understand words in their most concrete sense yields nonsense or some meaning inappropriate in context, then the words are being used figuratively.

Consider, for example, the first sentence of the domestic drama recounted above: "John sat at the breakfast table, buried deeply in the morning newspaper." That people are buried deeply is a fact of mortuary science; that they are buried deeply while sitting at the breakfast table is a strange idea. That there is enough mass in an ordinary morning paper to bury anything deeply is impossible. The phrase "buried deeply in the morning newspaper" is figurative speech.

The proverbs are littered with figurative speech similar to this. Proverbs 10:13 reads:

On the lips of the discerning, wisdom is found,

But a rod is for the back of him who lacks understanding.

To read all the words of this proverb in their most concrete sense would yield very odd and impossible notions. To find wisdom, we must locate discerning people and then search carefully on the pinkish, fleshy borders of their mouths. Admittedly, there are not many places to hide things on lips. But perhaps wisdom is tucked tightly into their corners or is teensy-weensy stuff hiding in the cracks and lines of lips. Clearly Proverbs 10:13 is speaking in figurative language!

When testing for figures in this way, you will often isolate words or expressions which appear to qualify as figures of speech but do not. An example is Proverbs 11:14:

Where there is no guidance, the people fall,

But in abundance of counselors there is victory.

If the words of this proverb are pressed to mean only the most concrete kind of affirmation, we would imagine that without guidance people literally fall—either falling down on the floor, or falling off their chairs or off other things on which they may be standing or sitting. In its most elementary and concrete sense, the verb *to fall* means to descend freely under the force of gravity. A consultation in a dictionary will reveal that dozens of similar meanings have developed from this concrete sense. Many or most of these meanings may have been figurative as they came into use in language. With long use, however, their figurative force has been lost. Such expressions are called *dead metaphors*.

As you become accustomed to isolating figures of speech in the proverbs, you will possibly locate many dead metaphors in addition to fully living figures of speech. Your ability to distinguish dead metaphors from live ones will only come through practice. Specific guidelines for identifying particular figures of speech—similes, direct and indirect metaphors, synecdoches and various metonymies—are given in successive chapters. With these guidelines and diligent practice, you will soon gain the discernment needed to recognize bona fide figures of speech.

Of course, proverbs can be expressed without figures of

speech. Proverbs 11:17 uses none at all:
The merciful man does himself good,
But the cruel man does himself harm.
In this proverb concrete nouns or verbs are used in their concrete senses without confusion or ambiguity. Abstract nouns may also be employed. In Proverbs 11:17, *the merciful man* and *the cruel man* denote concrete kinds of individuals with certain kinds of character. *Good* and *harm* are abstract nouns. No figures of speech are used in this proverb. Certain kinds of metonymy discussed in chapter ten employ abstract nouns, but these are not common.

Why Use Figures of Speech?
E. W. Bullinger's *Figures of Speech Used in the Bible* names, defines and gives examples of almost five hundred different figures of speech. C. Hugh Holman's *A Handbook to Literature* discusses fewer than fifty. Bullinger's work was published in 1898, Holman's in 1972. No judgments can be made concerning the skills which the man on the street may have in consciously understanding and employing figures of speech in Bullinger's day compared with modern English speakers. However, the standard reference works on literature in recent years have not approached Bullinger's zeal for thoroughness in cataloguing the various forms of figurative speech. This lack seems to correspond to several kinds of misunderstandings and confusions which modern readers have concerning figures of speech.

Some careless readers of the Bible, especially in its poetical sections, will dismiss some verse or paragraph or chapter with the words "Oh, that's just figurative language." By this they mean either "I don't know what this means" or "This does not mean anything at all in particular; it's just evocative language." Behind such a judgment on the figurative sections of the Bible lies another assumption—figurative language is easy to recognize. The assumption is incorrect. The apocalyptic literature of the Bible and some of the prophetic literature are florid with figures, but figures of speech are extremely common in all parts of the Bible. The purely literal portions of Scripture—that is, those portions which employ no figures of speech whatever—are very small and rare.

Figures of speech have three characteristics which are commonly employed by speakers. Without these characteristics of figurative speech, human language would be hopelessly dull, confusing and burdensome.

Vividness. Because figures of speech arise for the most part from concrete nouns and verbs, they draw upon a world of sensory experience, real or imagined, through which even abstract ideas can be communicated. The vividness of many figures of speech aids in communication in two important ways. First, figures of speech enable a speaker to express strange, abstract or unknown ideas in terms of known experience. Second, figures of speech help to hold the attention of a reader or listener, assuring full communication. It is important to realize that in order for figures of speech to be vivid, they do not need to draw attention to themselves. Texts containing figures of speech which draw attention to themselves as figures of speech are either ostentatious or deliberately artistic.

Accuracy. Far from being vague, figures of speech greatly enhance precision in communication. Consider again the opening line of the domestic drama discussed previously: "John sat at the breakfast table, buried deeply in the morning newspaper." The text might have said that John was obscured from his wife's view by a thick section of the *City News* which he was holding up to eye level. "Buried deeply" tells us the same thing and much more, for it implies a certain hold which the paper has over him, a kind of absence of spirit which exceeds his physical obscurity. "To be buried in something" is almost an idiom in English for total absorption in whatever it is one is said to be buried in. To express the same notion in nonfigurative language would probably be far less precise.

Efficiency. Figures of speech are amazingly efficient mediums of communication. Consider once more our friend buried in the newspaper. A *complete* description of John in this state which fully detailed all his physical and mental traits which combine to equal being "buried deeply in the morning newspaper," a description which employed no figures of speech whatsoever, would run into dozens and dozens of words. By using figures of speech an author can pack the greatest amount of information into the fewest words.

From these characteristics of figurative language, certain consequences follow for the users and hearers of figures of speech. A skilled communicator uses figures of speech deliberately to accomplish a specific goal. For the author of some text which contains a figure of speech, the figure itself has a very specific meaning and none other. It is a meaning which he or she intends us to reproduce in our minds as we hear or read the text containing the figure of speech. Texts which contain figures of speech are not malleable things which can be "interpreted" to mean just any old thing. It is our responsibility to handle the text in such a way as to ensure that the author's meaning is the one sought.

Figures of Speech in the Proverbs of Solomon

Proverbs and figures of speech have common roots embedded in the same soil. Concrete language lies at the root of most figures of speech, and concrete events—the stuff of human experience—give rise to most proverbs. It should come as no surprise that proverbs frequently employ figures of speech in highly artful and complicated ways in order to express some maxim. Even as some proverbs are so crafted as to exploit fully the meaning potential of parallelisms, so some proverbs make highly innovative use of figures of speech. When different figures of speech lie on opposite sides of a parallelism, the interpretive problems can become quite complex. Of course, not all proverbs are difficult or have obscure figurative language; many proverbs have no figures of speech at all. However, for those who are advanced along the way of wisdom, there are proverbs in Solomon's collection to tax all their acquired skills.

In the discussions of succeeding chapters, the most common figures of speech will be described, discussed and illustrated with examples. Perhaps one of the most common figures, however, will not be discussed since it is used for purposes of style rather than to convey some particular meaning. That figure, called *antimereia,* is the use of one part of speech for another. This figure of speech appears most often in the form of adjectives, such as *righteous, wicked, foolish, naive, diligent,* preceded by an article. For example, Proverbs 14:20 reads:

The poor is hated even by his neighbor,
But those who love the rich are many.

By *the poor* and *the rich* the proverb intends to mean the poor *person,* the rich *person.* When testing for figures in the proverbs, these figures may be ignored.

Study Questions: Chapter Seven

1. Reread carefully the domestic drama on page 82. Note the words which are figurative in the order in which they occur in the text. Indicate briefly after each figurative word or phrase *how* you can tell it is figurative.

2. Read carefully the following proverbs, and divide them into two groups: those which contain figures of speech and those which do not.

☐ He who speaks truth tells what is right,
But a false witness, deceit. (12:17)

☐ There is one who speaks rashly like the thrusts of a sword,
But the tongue of the wise brings healing. (12:18)

☐ Wealth obtained by fraud dwindles,
But the one who gathers by labor increases it. (13:11)

☐ The heart knows its own bitterness,
And a stranger does not share its joy. (14:10)

☐ The naive believes everything,
But the prudent man considers his steps. (14:15)

☐ A scoffer does not love one who reproves him,
He will not go to the wise. (15:12)

☐ Righteous lips are the delight of kings,
And he who speaks right is loved. (16:13)

☐ A servant who acts wisely will rule over a son who acts
    shamefully,
And will share in the inheritance among brothers. (17:2)

☐ Excellent speech is not fitting for a fool;
Much less are lying lips to a prince. (17:7)

☐ The words of a man's mouth are deep waters;
The fountain of wisdom is a bubbling brook. (18:4)

☐ The poor man utters supplications,
But the rich man answers roughly. (18:23)

☐ A king who sits on the throne of justice
Disperses all evil with his eyes. (20:8)

[CHAPTER EIGHT]

Your Hair Is Like a Flock of Goats: Similes & Metaphors

LOVERS HAVE BEEN PRAISING one another ever since the time there were lovers. Not many women, however, have been offered praise from their lover such as this:

How beautiful you are, my darling, how beautiful you are! Your hair is like a flock of goats descending a mountain, your teeth are like newly shorn ewes which have been dipped, your neck is a stone tower, hung with a thousand shields.

These words strike us as a very odd form of praise. Shaggy goats or shorn and dipped ewes might qualify as comic figures, but hardly as amorous ones. Yet, these comparisons are recorded in one of the oldest love songs in human literature—the Song of Solomon. The odd comparisons above are taken from chapter 4.

Brief scanning of the Song of Solomon reveals that most of

what each lover says to the other is cast in comparisons. This, in itself, is common enough. The unusual aspect of the Song of Solomon arises from the strange and unfamiliar things to which the lovers liken one another.

The most common figures of speech are those which make comparisons. The proper understanding of these figures— how they are composed, how they function, how they convey meaning—is essential if we are to grasp the message conveyed through the figure of speech. That comparisons have a determinate meaning is evident from the reaction people have to comparisons which they either do not understand or misunderstand. A modern young woman would probably not understand her boyfriend's comparing her hair to a flock of goats; she would probably think it was a jest or even an insult. We must assume, of course, that Solomon's Shulammite maiden understood his comparison and received it as praise. All of this reinforces the fact that comparisons are employed in order to communicate information. But if you are to accurately receive the information which comparisons are intended to convey, then you must understand how comparisons work.

Three Kinds of Comparison
Comparisons can be made in three ways. The easiest kind of comparison to make and understand is called a *simile*. In a simile two elements are compared by using words such as *like, alike, as* and *resemble*. "Your hair is like a flock of goats" affirms a resemblance between someone's hair and a flock of goats. Strictly speaking, a simile is not a figure of speech, for in a simile all the words can be understood *and are intended to be understood* concretely. However, because the meanings of similes are identical to other comparing figures of speech, they are classified as figures of speech along with other figures which make comparisons.

A second way in which comparisons can be made is by

equation. If a lover were to say to his beloved, "Your hair is a flock of goats," he would be using a figurative equation called a *metaphor*. In a metaphor both elements of the comparison are explicitly stated, and the fact that they are being compared is obvious. A metaphor is clearly a figure of speech, for the words of a metaphor cannot be understood concretely without yielding a meaning which is either nonsensical or fantastic.

A third and less obvious type of comparison is called a *hypocatastasis* (pronounced hypo-ca-TAS-tasis). In a hypocatastasis only one of the elements of the comparison is mentioned. It is assumed that the reader or hearer will understand the identity of the other element. For example, consider a comparison between *love* and *wine*. As long as both elements of the comparison are mentioned, the figure of speech employed is simply a simile or metaphor: "Your love is like wine" (simile); "Your love is strong dark wine" (metaphor). However, in the following statement one of the elements (love) is not stated: "I long for your strong dark wine, so that I may drink and forget my loneliness" (hypocatastasis). It is assumed that the reader or hearer will understand that *strong dark wine* is being compared to love.

These three comparing figures differ in the ease with which they are understood. Similes announce themselves explicitly. Metaphors are also not difficult to recognize as long as the equated elements are normally thought to be unequatable in a concrete sense. A hypocatastasis can be misunderstood, however, if there is insufficient context to make clear what is being assumed in the hypocatastasis. "I long for your strong dark wine" makes perfect concrete sense if spoken by someone approaching the bar of a saloon. However, in the context of intimate conversation between two lovers, it would not likely be understood as a concrete request for a drink of some dark-colored, fermented beverage made from grapes.

Comparisons in the Proverbs

Similes are as easy to identify in the proverbs as they are in any speech. Similes almost invariably employ the word *like* in the proverbs of Solomon. Two examples are Proverbs 12:18 and 16:15:

There is one who speaks rashly like the thrusts of a sword,
But the tongue of the wise brings healing.

In the light of a king's face is life,
And his favor is like a cloud with the spring rain.

In 12:18a speech is likened to the thrusting of a sword, while in 16:15b the king's favor is likened to a cloud. Very often in the proverbs the translators will render metaphors in the Hebrew text as similes in the English version. In the New American Standard Bible, for example, Proverbs 17:14 reads:

The beginning of strife is *like* letting out water,
So abandon the quarrel before it breaks out.

It is the usual custom of most English versions to italicize the words in the English text which have no corresponding word in the original text. Metaphors which are smooth in Hebrew may be excessively harsh in English, and these are frequently rendered as similes instead of metaphors.

Metaphors are usually simple to recognize in the proverbs, as they have the form "A is B" in circumstances where A is manifestly *not* B in a concrete sense. It is also common to find a metaphor in one line of a proverb and a simile in the other line. For example, Proverbs 18:11 is a synonymous parallelism containing both a simile and a metaphor:

A rich man's wealth is his strong city,
And like a high wall in his own imagination.

The first line of Proverbs 18:11 equates wealth and a strong city. In concrete terms wealth is *not* a city. However, the equation of the two affirms in a vivid way that wealth and a strong city have something in common, that they are alike. The second line of the proverb makes the same point, except a different image is set forth and a simile is employed instead of a metaphor. The rich man's wealth is said to be like a high wall. A strong city with a high wall affords protection for those who take refuge in it; so also does wealth provide security for those who take refuge in it. The wry addition of *in his own imagination* at the end of the second line suggests that the similarities are simply the viewpoint of the rich man and may not reflect the actual state of the matter.

Proverbs 12:4, on the other hand, is an antithetical parallelism which contains a simile and a metaphor:

An excellent wife is the crown of her husband,

But she who shames him is as rottenness in his bones.

The first line equates the excellent wife with a crown. As wives and crowns are not identical things, we know that this is a metaphor. The second line affirms that a wife who shames her husband is *like* rottenness in his bones. Both lines are asserting comparisons; one uses a metaphor, the other a simile. The pairing of similes and metaphors in the parallelisms of the proverbs is a very common phenomenon.

Proverbs 15:19 is an example of a dead metaphor being coupled with a "live" one:

The way of the sluggard is as a hedge of thorns,

But the path of the upright is a highway.

The word *as* in the first line indicates a simile; however, in the second line a path is equated with a highway. *Way* and *path* in this proverb are dead metaphors. In very concrete terms, a way or a path is some kind of track or course on which people travel. But because of the habitual, recurring nature of travel along a path or a way, the words *path* and *way*, in both English and Hebrew, have come to mean a characteristic, habitual kind of thought or action. A person's characteristic behavior is his *way*. "He really has a way with his patients" might be said of a doctor whose manner with his patients is comforting. In Proverbs 15:19, when the *way of the sluggard* or the *path of the upright* is mentioned, the writer means the customary behavior of these kinds of people. However, because of the repeated use of these expressions for behavior, they have lost their figurative flavor. Still, to equate the path of the upright with a highway is to affirm an equation which is not concretely true.

Hypocatastases in the proverbs often stand out glaringly; at other times they may be completely overlooked. Among hypocatastases which are easy to recognize is Proverbs 20:26:

A wise king winnows the wicked,

And drives the threshing wheel over them.

In concrete terms a wise king does nothing of the sort. While an especially cruel king might conceivably punish the wicked by crushing them under a threshing wheel, it is not possible to *winnow* human beings even if they are wicked. Winnowing is a process in which worthless material is separated from valuable material, especially as in the separation of grain from chaff. Proverbs 20:26 makes sense if we understand it to assume a comparison between a wise king and a man winnowing grain on one hand, and a comparison between the wicked and the grain to be winnowed on the other. Because this comparison is assumed in the proverb and not stated explicitly, Proverbs 20:26 is an example of a hypocatastasis. The point of the proverb is to be sought in the comparison. Even as harvested grain contains valuable and worthless material which needs to be separated, so the words, thoughts and deeds of the wicked man contain both worthless and valuable things which it is the business of a king to discern and separate. Driving the threshing wheel over the newly harvested grain is a means of rendering it amenable to winnowing. Evidently we are to understand that the king applies some sort of pressure to the wicked to make them amenable to the discerning justice of the wise king. We see a clear example of this process in 1 Kings 3:16-28. The testimonies of the two harlots concerning their possession of a child were clearly a mixture of truth and lies. Solomon "drove the threshing wheel over them" in proposing that the disputed child be cut into two pieces, to be divided between the mothers. Their reactions revealed who was the true mother.

The images of Proverbs 20:26 are so vivid and unusual that the hypocatastasis is easy to recognize. In many other proverbs, however, they can be overlooked. Proverbs 29:8, for example, states:

Scorners set a city aflame,
But wise men turn away anger.

The first line of this proverb, if read concretely, informs us that scorners are arsonists who burn down cities. This rather odd idea evaporates and the genuine sense of the statement emerges, however, as we understand "setting something on fire" to mean arousing it emotionally. *To burn* at someone or something is to be angry at them. Setting a city aflame in this sense would mean to provoke widespread anger and hostility, which is supported by the second line of the proverb. "Wise men turn away anger" is the contrast of the first line, and anger in the second line is to be understood concretely.

The difficulty with the implied comparison between anger and flame in Proverbs 29:8 is that it can be easily overlooked. To speak of anger as if it were a process of combustion is common enough in both Hebrew and English; consequently, such a hypocatastasis might go unnoticed in a rapid consideration of the proverb.

What Do Comparisons Mean?

You may realize at this point that one class of parallelism is built solely on these figures of speech which make comparisons. The emblematic parallelisms discussed in chapter five are nothing more or less than similes and metaphors. The discussion in chapter five concerning the meaning of emblematic proverbs and how to ascertain that meaning is completely applicable to any simile, metaphor or hypocatastasis in the book of Proverbs, with some minor adjustments.

As is true in emblematic parallelisms, any comparison is an assertion of partial identity. To say that A is like B is to affirm that A has some characteristics or traits in common with B. They do not, of course, have all their traits in common, for they would then be virtually identical. Only when they have some and only some characteristics in common does one become a possible emblem for the other.

The scope of the common traits between the things which are said to be alike is almost never expressed in a simile, metaphor or hypocatastasis. Therefore, behind each comparison in the proverbs lies the question, How is this like that? Every comparison is an invitation to explicate the traits which the two things have in common. In many proverbs you must interpret the comparison before you can understand the complete message of the proverb. Consider, for example, Proverbs 17:14:

The beginning of strife is like letting out water,
So abandon the quarrel before it breaks out.

Letting out water very likely means the accidental or intentional release of dammed water so that it flows out of its reservoir. Those who have watched children play with mud and garden hoses know the elements of hydrodynamics which this proverb speaks about. *The beginning of strife* and *letting out water* have the following traits in common:

1. They both may be very small at the beginning. Whether small or large at the beginning, they inevitably grow larger as they continue. Even a very small beginning is sufficient to bring the cataclysm if it is not corrected.

2. Untended leaks, like unchecked strife, grow larger with time, not smaller. Leaks never just "go away," and neither do quarrels.

3. There comes a time when neither a breach in a dam nor a quarrel may be reversed or repaired. Even before that time is

reached, all the water which has been released cannot be retrieved; neither can harsh words be recalled once they are spoken.

The point of this comparison is to warn us of the consequences of letting a quarrel run unchecked. The second half of the proverb urges the abandoning of the quarrel in light of the warning contained in the comparison of the first line.

As is true with emblematic parallelisms, the comparisons which these figures of speech make will be opaque if you have no knowledge of the image in the comparison. Those who have never witnessed the effects of a leak on an earthen dam will only dimly perceive the point of the proverb. Proverbs 18:10 tells us that "the name of the LORD is a strong tower." However, it has been some time since towers had much significance in the defensive strategies of warfare. Therefore, something of the vividness and significance of Proverbs 18:10 is missed by modern readers if they do not school themselves in the nature and function of towers in ancient warfare.

Parallelisms can interact with similes, metaphors and hypocatastases in various ways which will aid you in rightly discerning both parallelisms and comparisons. Sometimes, for example, there will be a comparison in one line and no figure of speech in another line, so that the point of the comparison may be isolated by reference to the nonfigurative part of the proverb. Proverbs 29:8a speaks of scorners setting a city aflame; when 29:8b speaks of wise men turning away anger, we are encouraged to understand the flames of the first line to be an implied comparison of fire with anger and hostility.

When there are comparisons in both lines of a proverb, they may be similar or different. When the comparisons are similar, they help to interpret one another and may shed light on the parallelism of the proverb. In Proverbs 20:26, for example, we saw that the winnowing/threshing comparison is assumed throughout the proverb. Similarly, in Proverbs

18:4 two kinds of water serve as emblems in metaphors:
The words of a man's mouth are deep waters;
The fountain of wisdom is a bubbling brook.
Deep waters and bubbling brooks are both kinds of naturally occurring waters. However, their differences far outnumber their similarities, which suggests that the proverb is an antithetical parallelism.

The emblems in the metaphors of Proverbs 15:19 are also contrasts. A hedge of thorns is an impediment to movement, while a highway facilitates movement. The way of a sluggard, therefore, is that which actually hinders accomplishment of some project, while the way of the upright greatly facilitates progress.

Occasionally some proverb will employ comparisons which do not seem to be drawn from the same spheres, as in Proverbs 12:4:
An excellent wife is the crown of her husband,
But she who shames him is as rottenness in his bones.
A crown and rottenness in the bones do not form good contrasts. Ordinarily you would need to flesh out the implied contrasts of this proverb. It would be best, however, to explicate the figures of speech before this explication of the suppressed contrasts is carried out. In general, it is best to unravel the figure of speech before unraveling any implied meanings in the parallelisms.

Study Questions: Chapter Eight

1. Read carefully the proverbs which are listed below. Identify any similes, metaphors and hypocatastases. In some proverbs there is one comparing figure of speech in the first line and a different one in the second line, even though the same emblem is being employed. (There are other figures of speech than similes, metaphors and hypocatastases. Do not identify these.)

☐ The rich man's wealth is his fortress,
   The ruin of the poor is their poverty. (10:15)
☐ Like vinegar to the teeth and smoke to the eyes,
   So is the lazy one to those who send him. (10:26)
☐ The way of the LORD is a stronghold to the upright,
   But ruin to the workers of iniquity. (10:29)
☐ The heart of the wise teaches his mouth,
   And adds persuasiveness to his lips. (16:23)
☐ Pleasant words are a honeycomb,
   Sweet to the soul and healing to the bones. (16:24)
☐ The words of a whisperer are like dainty morsels,
   And they go down into the innermost parts of the body.
      (18:8)
☐ He also who is slack in his work
   Is brother to him who destroys. (18:9)
☐ A brother offended is harder to be won than a strong city,
   And contentions are like the bars of a castle. (18:19)
☐ The king's wrath is like the roaring of a lion,
   But his favor is like dew on the grass. (19:12)
☐ He who is gracious to a poor man lends to the LORD,
   And He will repay him for his good deed. (19:17)

2. List five traits which a rich man's wealth and a fortress have in common.

3. List ten traits which are shared between the words of a whisperer and dainty morsels. Imagine your favorite dainty morsel as an aid in meditation (a petit four, a Christmas cookie, an elaborate hors d'oeuvre).

[CHAPTER NINE]

All about Parts & Wholes: Synecdoches

ALL THE MAJOR FIGURES OF speech you will encounter in the proverbs of Solomon operate according to one of two devices: comparison and substitution. The figures of speech discussed in the previous chapter—simile, metaphor and hypocatastasis—all operate by comparison. The figures discussed in this chapter and the next all operate by substitution: one word is substituted for another because of some relationship between the things designated by the words. When that relationship entails A being a part of B, and A is spoken of as though it were B, then the resulting figure of speech is a *synecdoche* (pronounced sin-NECK-dough-key).

Synecdoches are very common in spoken language. When we speak of turning on a light, we are using a synecdoche. What we are actually turning on is a lamp, or a light bulb or an overhead light fixture. A car may be spoken of as a motor, though the motor is only a part of the car. Dr. Knowsalot might be the best head on the faculty. A hired hand (worker) who desires to keep bread (food) on the table, a roof (shelter) over his family and a shirt (clothing) on his back (body) saddles up every morning (leaves for work by riding a horse) and puts in long hours (a work day) riding the range (his employer's property on which the cattle dwell). It is common to speak of persons and things by referring to one of their parts. This figure of speech is quite common in the proverbs.

Synecdoche in the Proverbs

Synecdoches are not hard to recognize in the proverbs if their concrete meanings are pressed. To understand a synecdoche in concrete terms invariably yields nonsense. Proverbs 10:27, for example, reads:

The fear of the LORD prolongs life,
But the years of the wicked will be shortened.

Years is a synecdoche for lifetime or life span. If 10:26b were understood concretely, it would mean that the wicked person's calendar had fewer days or months in it than anyone else's calendar. Proverbs 15:15 uses a similar measure of time to mean the span of a person's life:

All the days of the afflicted are bad,
But a cheerful heart has a continual feast.

Days of the afflicted is referring to the total time during which a person is afflicted.

Bread is a common synecdoche for food, as in Proverbs 12:11 and 22:9:

He who tills his land will have plenty of bread,
But he who pursues vain things lacks sense.

He who is generous will be blessed,
For he gives some of his bread to the poor.

The New American Standard Bible in Proverbs 22:9b actually translates the Hebrew word *lechem* as "food," though it means "bread," as the translation above reflects.

The most common synecdoches in the proverbs, however, are those in which persons are spoken about through terms which are the names of parts of their bodies. We have noted the use of the word *hand* to denote a hired worker. Hebrew employs *hand* in a similar fashion to indicate a working man, as in Proverbs 12:24:

The hand of the diligent will rule,
But the slack hand will be put to forced labor.

Head is also used to denote an individual, as in Proverbs 11:26 and 25:21-22:

He who withholds grain, the people will curse him,
But blessing will be on the head of him who sells it.

If your enemy is hungry, give him food [literally, *bread*]
    to eat;
And if he is thirsty, give him water to drink;
For you will heap burning coals on his head,
And the LORD will reward you.

These verses contain other figures of speech besides synecdoche. *Heap burning coals of fire on his head* is a complex figure. *Head* is a synecdoche for the enemy; *heaping burning coals* on that enemy is a hypocatastasis which has been understood in various senses—predominately as either judgment or shame, which are implicitly compared to the experience of having fire placed on one's person.

Some of the more interesting and difficult synecdoches are those denoting various psychological states or processes which an individual exhibits. These synecdoches employ terms such as *eyes, ears* and *heart*. Proverbs 17:24 uses the term *eyes* in an interesting synecdoche:

Wisdom is in the presence of him who has understanding,
But the eyes of a fool are on the ends of the earth.

The second line of this proverb describes a fool who is searching frantically far and wide for a way to get something accomplished, in contrast to a man of understanding who has wisdom in his presence at all times. The proverb says that the *eyes* of the fool search for a solution to some problem he is facing. *Eyes* becomes a quasi-psychological term for "searching attention." *Ends of the earth* is another synecdoche, in which the extreme horizons refer to everywhere in between them.

A proverb employing *eyes* in a different way is Proverbs 20:8:

A king who sits on the throne of justice
Disperses all evil with his eyes.

The New American Standard Bible translates the verb in 20:8 as "disperses," though the same verb appears in 20:26 and is rendered there as "winnows." Evidently the translation committee judged the idea of winnowing the wicked with one's eyes as too strange a notion for English ears. But even the idea of dispersing evil with one's eyes requires some explication, since in concrete terms such an idea is nonsense. This proverb speaks of the king's ability to discern between good and evil, his practiced "eye" which "sees" through those who are evil. *Eyes* becomes a term for "discernment." From this meaning for *eyes* it is a short step to the use of *eyes* to denote "settled opinion," as in Proverbs 12:15:

The way of a fool is right in his own eyes,
But a wise man is he who listens to counsel.

As the fool "looks at things," his way is correct; the wise man, however, has learned not to trust in the way things appear to him, so he seeks the counsel of others.

Ear becomes a term for things other than the concrete physical organ of hearing. In Proverbs 23:9, for example, it refers to the process of hearing itself:

Do not speak in the ears of a fool,
For he will despise the wisdom of your words.
Both the NASB and the RSV give the interpretive translation
"do not speak in the *hearing* of a fool," although the word
translated "hearing" is the Hebrew word for *ears*. Proverbs
15:31 uses *ears* to denote "listening attentively":
He whose ear listens to the life-giving reproof
Will dwell among the wise.
Some expressions involving *ear* mean "Pay attention!" as in
Proverbs 22:17:
Incline your ear and hear the words of the wise,
And apply your mind to my knowledge.
In the second half of this verse the word *mind* is actually trans-
lating the Hebrew word *leb*, which means "heart," one of the
most versatile synecdoches in all Scripture.

Modern English invests *heart* with a psychological sense
in many ways far removed from its meaning in the Bible.
Webster's New Collegiate Dictionary indicates that the use of
the word *heart* to denote "intellect" is obsolete. Rather *heart*
denotes "the emotional or moral nature as distinguished
from the intellectual nature." *The Reader's Digest Great En-
cyclopedic Dictionary* defines *heart* in its psychological sense
as "the seat of emotion, especially of love and affection, as
distinguished from the head, the center of intellect and reason." These definitions of *heart* will not reflect the Bible's use
of that term for two reasons. First, the Bible's use of *heart* is
very broad, covering such aspects as the will, emotions, the
mind and conscience. The heart in Proverbs exhibits all these
aspects. And second, the Bible gives no evidence of a dis-
tinction between the seat of the intellect and the emotive part
of human personality.

Heart in Proverbs can denote the emotive aspects of a person. The heart can be weighted down with anxiety (Prov
12:25; 25:20). It can be sick with disappointment (13:12), bit-
ter (14:10) and envious (23:17). The heart can also be merry

(15:13; 17:22) and glad (24:17; 27:11).

In addition to these emotive capacities of the heart there are capacities of the will. The heart can trust (28:26), or it can become hardened (28:14). The heart can exhibit pathological spiritual conditions such as perverseness (11:20; 12:8), deceit (12:20), backsliding (14:14) and pride (16:5). On the other hand, the heart can be clean (20:9) or pure (22:11). The heart can be imbued with folly (22:15) or with wisdom (10:8; 11:29). All these capacities and operations of the heart involve exercises of volition, responsible choices which may be evaluated by a moral standard.

Where human intellectual capacities are concerned, the word *heart* in Proverbs parts company with the meaning of *heart* in modern American English. As we have seen, contemporary meanings for *heart* entail a specific exclusion of intellectual operations. In the Proverbs, however, the heart seeks knowledge (15:14), studies (15:28), plans and devises (16:9), teaches (16:23) and learns (18:15). The heart may be applied to knowledge (22:17) and instruction (23:12). The RSV in all these places translates the Hebrew *leb* by "mind" rather than "heart," and in only three of the above listed references does the NASB render *leb* by "heart" (15:28; 16:23; 23:12), translating it as "mind" in the other instances. As you study the proverbs in the English versions, therefore, beware of importing into the word *heart* the meaning which you have grown up with. The narrowness of the meaning of *heart* in English reduces its value in translation even in those places in the proverbs where *heart* denotes some emotive aspect of personality.

Another psychological term in Proverbs which has a meaning strange to modern occidental ears is the Hebrew word *nephesh*, usually rendered "soul." In modern English *soul* as a psychological term is understood as the immaterial part of a person's being, less often as the animating aspect of his being. The basic human paradigm in the Scripture, however, is given in Genesis 2:7. After Adam's body is formed from the earth, God breathes the breath of life into him and "man became a living soul" (KJV). This pattern is reflected in Ezekiel's vision of the dry bones in Ezekiel 37:5-6:

Thus says the Lord GOD to these bones, "Behold, I will cause breath [or "spirit"] to enter you that you may come to life. And I will put sinews on you, make flesh grow back on you, cover you with skin, and put breath ["spirit"] in you that you may come alive; and you will know that I am the LORD."

A soul, therefore, is the composite result of a spirit conjoined with a body. A person *has* a body and a spirit, but he or she *is* a soul.

Proverbs reflects this view in several ways. *Nephesh* will often be used in Hebrew for "self" or the reflexive pronouns "himself," "herself," "oneself." Compare, for example, the renderings of Proverbs 15:32 in the New American Standard Bible and the King James Version:

He that refuseth instruction despiseth his own soul:
but he that heareth reproof getteth understanding. (KJV)

He who neglects discipline despises himself,
But he who listens to reproof acquires understanding.
    (NASB)

These two proverbs affirm substantially the same ideas. However, "despiseth his own *soul*" (KJV) might lead you to ponder precisely what aspect or part of yourself you would be despising if you were to refuse instruction. This question would never have occurred to the original Hebrew readers. *Soul* indicates that *all of the person* is harmed by ignoring instruction.

Indeed, *soul* can mean "person" or "life," as in Proverbs 19:2 and 20:2:

Also it is not good for a *person* to be without knowledge,
And he who makes haste with his feet errs.

The terror of a king is like the growling of a lion;
He who provokes him to anger forfeits his own *life*.

When the proverbs speak of a person's immaterial aspect,
the word *spirit* is employed. Proverbs 18:14 makes an illum-
inating comment on the psychology of the proverbs:
  The spirit of a man can endure his sickness,
  But a broken spirit who can bear?
A person's spirit can bear the difficult aspects of life; but
when the *spirit* is broken, then the person is helpless indeed.
Because a person's spirit gives strength, definition and shape
to his character, it was seen to function toward his personality as the bones do to a body. The term *bones*, therefore,
became a synonym for spirit, as can be seen in Proverbs 12:4
and 16:24:

  An excellent wife is a crown to her husband,
  But she who shames him is as rottenness in his bones.

  Pleasant words are a honeycomb,
  Sweet to the soul and healing to the bones.

The Significance of Synecdoche
The use of synecdoche in proverbial literature arises naturally from the tendency of all proverbs to grow out of concrete
human experience. As human experience becomes distilled
into knowledge, the expression of that knowledge in speech
becomes abstract, further and further removed from human
experience, except where that speech falls back on figurative
language. That vast body of knowledge known as mathe-
matics has its roots in the comparison of the fingers of one's
hands to other objects. From this concrete fact of human ex-

perience arises base-ten number systems in every human culture on the face of the globe. It would be difficult, however, to see in an advanced textbook on differential equations the roots of that subject in a child's counting his fingers. The figures of speech that operate by comparison hedge the knowledge of the proverbs from evaporating into airy nonexperience. Synecdoches accomplish the same end by referring to some idea or thing by one of its elements, one of its parts, one of its particulars. Of all the major figures of speech in the proverbs, synecdoche is the one which most deliberately combats the generality of abstractions with particularity. Consider, for example, Proverbs 10:27:

The fear of the LORD prolongs life,
But the years of the wicked will be shortened.

The reference to *years* in the second line is a synecdoche for lifetime, life span or some similar notion. A lifetime, however, is an intangible thing. Our own lifetimes have no beginning *in our experience* and no ending. Even the lifetimes of those who are born and die while we are acquainted with them are not experienced as things with beginnings, ends and middles. We do, however, experience the cycles of time which compose a lifetime—years and days. Years have definitive beginnings which we experience repeatedly; they have seasons, holidays and anniversaries which mark their duration; they have conclusions and endings, all of which we experience repeatedly even in a short lifetime. Years can be counted and otherwise particularized. The statement "the lifetime of the wicked will be shortened" is a truth affirmed in Proverbs. To say "the years of the wicked will be shortened" affirms the same truth with the additional reminder that lifetimes, whether wicked or wise, are things which the God of all flesh measures and allots in discrete, numerable portions. It implies that he increases or decreases the years of those who fear or fail to fear him.

This particularizing function of synecdoche often serves to

focus our attention on some aspect or feature which is spoken of in the proverb. Proverbs 15:31, for example, tells us:

He whose ear listens to the life-giving reproof
Will dwell among the wise.

Of course the first line is speaking about a *person* who listens to reproof, not about someone's ear which listens more or less independently of the person whose ear it is. However, because the synecdoche speaks of this person by referring to his ear, our attention is focused on the activity of *listening* to life-giving reproof. The person spoken of in this proverb does not merely hear reproof, he "has an ear" for it, as if there were some part of him which was continually alert for life-giving reproof from any quarter.

For the same reasons, synecdoches can sometimes direct you to a concrete application, as in Proverbs 18:15:

The mind of the prudent acquires knowledge,
And the ear of the wise seeks knowledge.

Both the inner and outer person is employed when learning occurs. The mind (Heb. *leb*, "heart") receives and stores it, and the ear seeks it. Of course the ear does no such thing, in a concrete sense. It is the wise *person* who seeks knowledge. However, the synecdoche *ear* tells us that the wise person makes his search by listening to others. If we would be knowledgeable, we must listen as well.

Study Questions: Chapter Nine

1. Some of the following proverbs use the word *eye* as a synecdoche; others use it in a nonfigurative sense. Which proverbs employ *eye* as a synecdoche?

☐ He who winks the eye causes trouble,
And a babbling fool will be thrown down. (10:10)
☐ Like vinegar to the teeth and smoke to the eyes,
So is the lazy one to those who send him. (10:26)
☐ The way of a fool is right in his own eyes,
But a wise man is he who listens to counsel. (12:15)
☐ The eyes of the LORD are in every place,
Watching the evil and the good. (15:3)
☐ He who winks his eyes does so to devise perverse things;
He who compresses his lips brings evil to pass. (16:30)
☐ Who has woe? Who has sorrow? Who has contentions?
Who has complaining? Who has wounds without cause?
Who has redness of eyes? (23:29)
☐ Your eyes will see strange things,
And your mind will utter perverse things. (23:33)
☐ A man with an evil eye hastens after wealth,
And does not know that want will come upon him. (28:22)

2. Examine the following proverbs and identify the words in them which are synecdoches.

☐ The righteous has enough to satisfy his appetite,
But the stomach of the wicked is in want. (13:25)
☐ The naive believe everything,
But the prudent man considers his steps. (14:15)
☐ The mind of man plans his way,
But the LORD directs his steps. (16:9)
☐ A gray head is a crown of glory;
It is found in the way of righteousness. (16:31)
☐ Listen to counsel and accept discipline,
That you may be wise the rest of your days. (19:20)
☐ Judgments are prepared for scoffers,
And blows for the back of fools. (19:29)

[CHAPTER TEN]

Houses
That Talk:
Metonymies

BILLY'S FATHER LOOKED UP from his paper. Billy was wandering carefully and slowly out of the den into the hall, muttering softly, then pausing to listen intently in all directions at once.

"Billy, what are you doing?"

Looking little-boy annoyed, Billy pressed a pudgy finger against pursed lips. "Shhhhh, Daddy. I wanna hear the house talk."

"What? The house doesn't talk, Billy. It's just a house. Houses don't talk."

"But Aaron's house talks," Billy insisted. "The pastor said so; and the President's house talks all the time too, 'cause the man on the TV said so lots of times. I wanna hear the house talk."

Some close questioning by Billy's father revealed the source of Billy's confusion. That morning in worship, Billy had heard the pastor read Psalm 118:3—"O let the house of Aaron say, 'His lovingkindness is everlasting.' " This called up to Billy's mind the several times he had heard the TV newscaster say, "The White House said today..." If Pastor and the TV both said so, then houses could talk, and Billy wanted to hear his house talk too.

Billy's childish mind understood language at a very concrete level; hence his confusion about talking houses. Adults who are more practiced in standard figures of speech would never have misunderstood; it is doubtful they would even have sensed a figure of speech was being employed. However, both Billy and his father might be perplexed by the statement in Proverbs 10:11b, "The mouth of the wicked conceals violence." What might the violence look like if we were to peer into the wicked person's mouth to see what was concealed there? Talking houses, violence in wicked people's mouths, and a number of other strange-sounding notions begin to make regular sense when we understand the figure of speech known as *metonymy* (meh-TAWN-neh-mee).

Definition of Metonymy

In a synecdoche, discussed in the previous chapter, a word substitution takes place according to the relationship of a part to a whole—some person, thing, event or process is mentioned by employing the name of one of its parts or vice versa. However, the part-whole relationship is not the only one which can generate figures of speech through substitution. In general, A may be named by employing the word B if A and B have some demonstrable relationship between them. When this kind of substitution takes place in speech, the figure of speech is called a metonymy.

When one considers how metonymies function, their number is as large as there are relationships between things. However, in spite of elaborate classification schemes devised by rhetoricians, most metonymies fall into two large classes: cause-effect metonymies and subject-predicate metonymies.

Cause-Effect Metonymies

In a cause-effect metonymy, the substitution is governed by the relationship of cause and effect. A cause is mentioned for its effect, or an effect is mentioned for its cause.

Consider again Proverbs 10:11b: "The mouth of the wicked conceals violence." *Mouth* is a cause-effect metonymy, the mouth being mentioned instead of the words which the mouth produces. The mouth is an instrumental cause of the words which a person speaks. *Violence,* on the other hand, is an abstract noun denoting the effect which the words of the wicked achieve—usually violence for others. If we were to paraphrase this statement without employing these cause-effect metonymies, the idea would be expressed something like this: A wicked person's words are such as to conceal the violent deeds which he intends to accomplish. An example of such speech is found in Jezebel's plot to acquire Naboth's vineyard through a false accusation (1 Kings 21:7-15). She arranges to have two men accuse Naboth of cursing God and the king. Their accusation, apparently made to maintain religious and civil justice, actually conceals Jezebel's wicked intention to have Naboth killed so that her husband, King Ahab, can seize Naboth's vineyard.

Cause-effect metonymies account for many uses of abstract nouns in the proverbs. Furthermore, spiritual or psychological states are often mentioned in the proverbs in cause-effect metonymies. For example, Proverbs 10:21b tells us that "fools die for lack of understanding." If these words were simply and concretely true, if they were employing no figure of speech at all, then we would understand this statement to mean that lack of understanding is the sole, simple and direct cause of death. The ample supply of healthy fools in every place indicates that something more is involved. "Lack of understanding" is a metonymy of cause; the proverb mentions a psychological state which causes foolish behavior, which in turn leads to death. The tragic deaths of foolish people who overdose on drugs or die in automobile accidents under the influence of alcohol give sobering justification to the warning of Proverbs 10:21b.

Proverbs 18:7 tells us: "A fool's mouth is his ruin,/And his lips are the snare of his soul." In this proverb, *mouth* and *ruin* are not capable of being equated concretely, as *mouth* is a tangible part of the fool's body, while *ruin* is a wholly abstract concept. *Ruin* is very likely an effect of some behavior of the fool, behavior which has as its consequence the ruin of the fool. That behavior is specified by another cause-effect metonymy, *mouth*. The mouth is mentioned as the instrumental cause of the words which they produce. *Lips* in the second line is a similar cause-effect metonymy—the lips are mentioned rather than the words which they emit.

The majority of cause-effect metonymies in Proverbs employ concrete nouns which are mentioned as the instrumental causes of some particular effect. *Mouth* and *lips* are used in this way in the proverb mentioned above. Dozens of proverbs mention the mouth, tongue and lips rather than the words which they produce. In a similar way, Proverbs 10:4b tells us, "The hand of the diligent makes rich." *Hand* here is mentioned for the work which the hand does.

Subject-Predicate Metonymies
Subject-predicate metonymies function in the same way as any other metonymy—one word or idea is substituted for another according to some relationship between them. When the metonymy is the subject-predicate sort, then the words which appear in the figure express some quality, trait or attribute of the word or idea which does not appear because of the substitution. If B is a predicate of A, then B is mentioned instead of A in a subject-predicate metonymy.

A very common form of subject-predicate metonymy mentions the place or location of a thing when speaking of it. This subject-predicate metonymy accounts for talking houses, as when a news reporter tells us that the White House said so-and-so today. Most likely, the report was made by a presidential news secretary or some high official on the President's staff. However, because the White House is the President's residence and has become regularly associated in the public's mind with the office and the man who holds it, *the White House* is commonly mentioned in a subject-predicate metonymy for the man who resides in it.

House is also used in Proverbs in this sense, as in Proverbs 12:7:

The wicked are overthrown and are no more,
But the house of the righteous will stand.

If *house* is not a figure of speech, then this proverb tells us that the residential structures in which righteous people dwell are strong and enduring. However, *house* in this proverb actually is a subject-predicate metonymy for the righteous person's family—its members, institutions, customs and ways. The *house* is mentioned rather than the *household* which lives inside it.

A subject-predicate metonymy which sounds strange to modern ears employs the word *gates*. The gates of a city in biblical times were more than just entrances into the city through the walls around the city. Markets were held at the gates, with the major items sold giving their name to the gate (Sheep Gate, Neh 3:1; Fish Gate, Neh 3:3; Horse Gate, Neh 3:28). Even as monetary matters were concluded at the gates, so also legal and governmental matters were conducted there. This is the background of the warning in Proverbs 22:22-23:

Do not rob the poor because he is poor,
Or crush the afflicted at the gate;
For the LORD will plead their case,
And take the life of those who rob them.

In this warning, *gate* likely stands for the civil courts which were held by the elders of the city at the gates.

When a king rendered judgments, he would sit on his throne in a solemn convening of the royal court (for example, Esther 5:1). From this practice, *throne* came to be used for the king's authority, his reign or the judicial judgments which he handed down. Proverbs 16:12 tells us:

It is an abomination for kings to commit wickedness,
For a throne is established on righteousness.

Throne in this proverb is a subject-predicate metonymy. The place of the king's judicial activity is named for that activity which takes place when he sits on the throne.

There are many instances of subject-predicate metonymies in Proverbs which specify some activity in the figure of speech. This activity is mentioned in order to call to the reader's mind some other quality, trait, psychological state, purpose or activity of the person who performs the activity mentioned in the figure. For example, Proverbs 13:3 says:

The one who guards his mouth preserves his life;
The one who opens wide his lips comes to ruin.

If the phrase *opens wide his lips* is not figurative, then Proverbs 13:3b is telling us that the mere separating of one's jaws and the wide distention of the lips are ruinous. However, it is not difficult to see that "opening wide the lips" is an activity which is characteristic of one who speaks profusely, almost as if the words were a forceful torrent to be let out by getting the lips out of the way!

Proverbs 10:10a tells us that "he who winks the eye causes trouble." Again, blinking one eye quickly in and of itself cannot cause trouble. *Winking the eye* is a subject-predicate metonymy, an activity mentioned in order to evoke an image of a particular character or to suggest his wicked purpose. Proverbs 6:12-14 delineates that character and his purpose by mentioning the winking of the eye and other invidious behavior:

117

A worthless person, a wicked man,
Is the one who walks with a false mouth,
Who winks with his eyes, who signals with his feet,
Who points with his fingers;
Who with perversity in his heart devises evil continually,
Who spreads strife.

Confusion of Metonymy and Synecdoche

It is evident at this point that a synecdoche is really just a special kind of metonymy. In cause-effect metonymies a cause is mentioned instead of an effect, and vice versa. In a subject-predicate metonymy some characteristic, trait or activity is mentioned instead of the subject of which it may be predicated. A synecdoche is merely a part-whole metonymy in which a part is mentioned instead of the whole of which it is a part. For this reason, there are some metonymies in Proverbs—almost invariably employing some part of the body—which may prove troublesome to classify as either synecdoches or cause-effect metonymies. For example, Proverbs 10:20 says:

The tongue of the righteous is as choice silver,
The heart of the wicked is worth little.

Do we understand the word *heart* to be a synecdoche for the wicked person, or is it perhaps a cause-effect metonymy for the thoughts formed by the heart? The parallelism of Proverbs 10:20 helps somewhat. By *the tongue of the righteous*, the verse is probably speaking of the words which the righteous person speaks; *tongue* is the instrumental cause of the *words* which it produces. An appropriate contrast with "words which a righteous person says" would be "words which a wicked person says." When we find, however, that the second line speaks of "the heart of the wicked," we may still find here an appropriate contrast with the first line if we understand *heart* not as a synecdoche but as another metonymy, specifying the heart as the cause or source of the wicked person's thoughts and words. The implication of the second line would be that the wicked person's words are worthless because the heart which produces those words is worthless.

A similar thought is expressed in Proverbs 15:7, in which *heart* again appears not as a synecdoche, but as metonymy for the thoughts that proceed from the heart:

The lips of the wise spread knowledge,
But the hearts of fools are not so.

The lesson here is that the lips of the fool do not spread knowledge because his heart is incapable of formulating or containing it. Again, the clue that *heart* in Proverbs 15:7 is a metonymy comes from the parallelism with *lips* in the first line.

It is not so simple to decide between metonymy or synecdoche in Proverbs 12:19:

Truthful lips will be established forever,
But a lying tongue is only for a moment.

Truthful lips and *lying tongue* might signify "the man who speaks truly" and "the man who speaks falsely"; or, on the other hand, they may signify, by metonymy, "truthful words" and "lying words." If the latter is meant, the thought is that truth can never be controverted, while falsehood by contrast is only momentary, liable to controversion at any time. If it is the person who speaks that forms the subject of this proverb, then the idea is somewhat similar to that of Proverbs 19:5:

A false witness will not go unpunished,
And he who tells lies will not escape.

Either interpretation makes good sense, and it is difficult to insist that either of them is preferable over the other.

It was noted above that *tongue*, *lips* and *mouth* are very often cause-effect metonymies for the speech which these organs produce. Occasionally these organs of speech will be synecdoches, as in Proverbs 26:28:

A lying tongue hates those it crushes,
And a flattering mouth works ruin.

If *lying tongue* in the first line is speaking of speech composed of lies, then we must infer a further figure of speech to make *hating* a plausible activity of *speech*. It is much simpler to understand *lying tongue* as a synecdoche for a person who speaks lies. By parallelism, *flattering mouth* is probably a synecdoche for a person who speaks flattery.

Complex Figures

Mixing figures of speech is often prohibited by teachers of elementary composition. Such a prohibition evidently did not occur to the composers of the proverbs in Solomon's collection. Some proverbs present striking complexes of figures within figures.

Consider, for example, the first line of Proverbs 10:21: "The lips of the righteous feed many." *Lips* in this line is a common cause-effect metonymy for speech or words. *The lips of the righteous* would mean the words which a righteous man speaks. However, this is not the end of the figures, for there is still the implicit comparison between the speech of the righteous man and food. Righteous words can feed many only if we assume a hypocatastasis which compares speech to food. With this implicit comparison we are invited to ponder the various ways in which food and the words of the righteous are alike.

Another striking and complex figure is the first line of Proverbs 14:3: "In the mouth of the foolish is a rod for his back." Again, *mouth* is a cause-effect metonymy for "words" or "speech." A rod is a common implement of punishment; *rod for his back* is speaking of punishment through another cause-effect metonymy, *rod* being mentioned as an instrumental cause of the punishment which it inflicts. However, saying "in the fool's speech is punishment for him" would still be using figurative language. There is some intermediate assumption connecting the speech of a fool with his being punished. Very likely, we are to suppose that the fool's

speech, because it is foolish, contains or commits some transgression, as we read in Proverbs 24:9:
The devising of folly is sin,
And the scoffer is an abomination to men.
As there is criminal trespass in his speech, so he merits punishment, as we read in Proverbs 18:6:
A fool's lips bring strife,
And his mouth calls for blows.
Therefore, *a rod for his back* is not only a metonymy which signifies punishment; that punishment which it signifies is another cause-effect metonymy, the effect of the transgression which he commits in his speaking.

A Final Word on Figures

The explanation and illustration of figures of speech in the previous four chapters have pointed you many times to modes of speaking which were already familiar to you. While common speech may not display the density of figurative language that the proverbs display, nevertheless the figures of Solomon's proverbs are not alien to the man on the street. Indeed, language which contains no figures of speech is very rare, being confined for the most part to technical literature. To speak figuratively is to speak normally and colloquially.

Why then spend such labor in learning the kinds of figures, how they work and how they may be combined? One of the primary purposes of Solomon's collection is that we should learn "to understand a proverb and a figure, the words of the wise and their riddles" (Prov 1:6). The familiarity with figures of speech which we acquire from merely learning to speak does not necessarily facilitate our understanding of figurative language. In the hands of the wise, figures and riddles were raised to a level of art in the expression of wisdom. The wisdom which is locked in figures of speech is finally accessible only to those exercised in unlocking those figures. This mental purpose of Solomon's proverbs is not an end in itself, however. Beyond the skill of understanding figures and proverbs, wise sayings and riddles, lies wisdom itself, the real prize, who when she is found offers the ultimate reward:

If you seek her as silver,
And search for her as for hidden treasures;
Then you will discern the fear of the LORD,
And discover the knowledge of God. (Prov 2:4-5)

Study Questions: Chapter Ten

Identify the metonymies in the following proverbs by *(a)* specifying the word(s) in the metonymy, *(b)* naming the metonymy as either cause-effect or subject-predicate, and *(c)* explaining the sense of the metonymy.

☐ By the blessing of the upright a city is exalted,
But by the mouth of the wicked it is torn down. (11:11)

☐ The words of the wicked lie in wait for blood,
But the mouth of the upright will deliver them. (12:6)

☐ The wise woman builds her house,
But the foolish tears it down with her own hands. (14:1)

☐ The LORD will tear down the house of the proud,
But He will establish the boundary of the widow. (15:25)

☐ He who winks his eyes does so to devise perverse things;
He who compresses his lips brings evil to pass. (16:30)

☐ A foolish son is a grief to his father,
And bitterness to her who bore him. (17:25)

☐ Take away the wicked from before the king,
And his throne will be established in righteousness. (25:5)

☐ Like one who takes off a garment on a cold day, or like
vinegar on soda,
Is he who sings songs to a troubled heart. (25:20)

☐ A whip is for the horse, a bridle for the donkey,
And a rod for the back of fools. (26:3)

[CHAPTER ELEVEN]

Doing Wisdom: Application of Proverbs to Living

A THEME WHICH RECURS ALMOST monotonously in Proverbs 1—9 is the rewarding utility of wisdom. No more succinct statement of this theme can be cited than Proverbs 3:13-15:

How blessed is the man who finds wisdom,
And the man who gains understanding.
For its profit is better than the profit of silver,
And its gain than fine gold.
She is more precious than jewels;
And nothing you desire compares with her.

In succeeding verses Solomon details these rewards of wisdom: long life, riches and honor (v. 16); pleasure and peace (v. 17); life and joy (v. 18).

These rewards are not reserved merely for human investments of labor. God himself has found wisdom useful for his work from the time of creation (v. 19), a theme elaborated in

Proverbs 8:22-31. From the most august operations of God (v. 20) to the more ordinary obligations of man (v. 21), wisdom is a way of living which is essentially free from failure and fear (vv. 23-24).

The Range of Wisdom

Wisdom is not something to do; rather it is a way of doing things. This is borne out by the bewildering variety of human endeavors mentioned in the Old Testament in connection with wisdom.

For example, when the Lord is giving Moses instructions for the construction of the tabernacle, its equipment, and the clothes and utensils for the priests, wisdom is mentioned time after time in connection with those who perform the labor. God directs Moses in Exodus 28:3 to "speak to all the skillful persons [literally, "wise of heart"] whom I have endowed with the spirit of wisdom, that they make Aaron's garments." Wisdom, therefore, pertains to sewing garments. In Exodus 31:1-11 the Lord singles out Bezalel and Oholiab to lead guilds of workmen who are "wise of heart" for working in jewelry, cutting precious stones, wood carving, furniture making, casting of gold and bronze implements, weaving and perfumery. A similar list of crafts is mentioned in Exodus 35:30-35.

Handicrafts are not the only endeavors which display wisdom. Joseph displayed his wisdom to Pharaoh in the interpretation of dreams (Gen 41:38-39). Pharaoh saw that he would also have the wisdom to manage Egypt's agricultural production in preparation for the coming famine (Gen 41:33-36, 40-42). King Solomon displayed his wisdom in a variety of areas—the administration of justice (1 Kings 3:28), botany and biology (1 Kings 4:33) and statesmanship (1 Kings 5:12). Solomon even excelled in the pursuit and acquisition of wisdom (1 Kings 4:29-32), leaving behind him in the Old Testament canon not only the book of Proverbs, but also Ecclesiastes and the Song of Solomon.

Whether it is the management of a domestic political crisis (Esther 1:13-22), the efficient management of a domicile (Prov 14:1; 31:10-31) or even so simple a matter as chopping wood (Eccles 10:10), wisdom has the advantage of giving success to those who possess it. Whatever you do can be done with wisdom. Conversely, wisdom is invariably displayed in concrete, practical living. Wisdom is *skill*; to be wise is to have skill in living.

How to Chop Wood

Where then in the book of Proverbs does one find wisdom about woodchopping? One such place is Proverbs 13:20:

He who walks with wise men will be wise,

But the companion of fools will suffer harm.

If this proverb appears to have nothing at all to do with woodchopping, such appearances likely arise from modern unbiblical notions concerning wisdom and wise men. *Webster's New Collegiate Dictionary*, for example, records two meanings for *wise man:* "(1) a man of unusual learning, judgment, or insight: sage (2) a man versed in esoteric lore (as of magic or astrology)." The missing definition—missing because it is a biblical sense of the word and not a contemporary one—is "a man with skill or dexterity in some technique or trade." If this is what the proverbs mean by a wise man, then Proverbs 13:20 tells us how to acquire wisdom in woodchopping —go to a man who already has that wisdom, a man who is skilled in chopping wood, to learn from him.

Proverbs 13:20 gives us far more, of course, than advice on chopping wood. It directs us toward those who are wise in whatever area we desire to acquire wisdom, whether it be the building of ships or model airplanes, the administration of a nation or the conducting of a birthday party for toddlers. Furthermore, the breadth of scope in the applicability of this proverb is quite typical of the proverbs in Solomon's collection. They are rarely narrow in scope or subject matter.

There are some proverbs, however, which appear to be quite specific in scope or subject matter. One example is Proverbs 26:15:

The sluggard buries his hand in the dish;
He is weary of bringing it to his mouth again.

This proverb gives us a comical picture of the thorough commitment to laziness which a sluggard displays. Though the picture is comic, the significance is tragic—a sluggard would choose to go without food rather than do that very task which would feed him. But even in so specific a proverb as this one, there are applications beyond its immediate import. It teaches us, for example, that need does not motivate a sluggard, for even the most pressing and selfish need is insufficient to motivate a sluggard to work.

Proverbs 10:19 is another proverb with a specific subject which has wide applicability:

When there are many words, transgression is unavoidable,
But he who restrains his lips is wise.

In one sense the application of this proverb is narrow—be very slow to speak; take pains to actually restrain yourself from speaking. On the other hand, the application of this proverb is almost limitless, for it places no limits on the circumstances in which it is wise to refrain from speaking. In virtually every situation where one might speak, Proverbs 10:19 counsels restraint.

It may even happen that a proverb with extreme specificity in subject matter may have broad applicability. Consider Proverbs 11:1:

A false balance is an abomination to the LORD,
But a just weight is His delight.

Proverbs 16:11 and 20:10 are similar in import:

A just balance and scales belong to the LORD;
All the weights of the bag are His concern.

Differing weights and differing measures,
Both of them are abominable to the LORD.

These proverbs insist that the Lord has an intense interest in
the process and paraphernalia of weights and measures. The
Lord is not unmoved by what transpires on the butcher's or
grocer's scales. But is he concerned about gas pumps, a measuring device unknown to Israel's wise men? Most likely so,
for it would appear incongruous to suppose God is concerned with some methods of measurement to the exclusion
of others. It seems on further reflection that it is not really the
method of measuring which is of so intense concern to him
as it is that the measurements be just and stable. If ever we
ask "why?" these proverbs turn us to God himself for the
answer. Because he is just and stable, because he is the measure of all things, then all scales and balances become finite
replicas of something infinite and eternal in him. With this
consideration, the applicability of Proverbs 11:1, 16:11 and
20:10 rapidly expands beyond merely tangible objects and
measurements. Any standard of valuation or measurement
and any process of applying that standard become a concern
to the Lord. Only the sphere of application in these proverbs
differs from the statement of Proverbs 17:15:
He who justifies the wicked, and he who condemns the
    righteous,
Both of them alike are an abomination to the LORD.
The majority of Solomon's proverbs are general in subject
matter, and this has often been their most frustrating feature
to new students of the proverbs. Proverbs 12:1, for example,
reads:
Whoever loves discipline loves knowledge,
But he who hates reproof is stupid.
Discipline and reproof are abstract concepts in this proverb,
and it is difficult to conceive of them as objects of love and
hate. A proverb like this begins to yield its wisdom only

when you make the effort to concretize the general principle or abstract idea contained in the proverb. To do this try imagining or recalling specific events or situations which embody the truth which the proverb expresses. The final payoff will come when you succeed in finding *in your own circumstances* an opportunity to concretize the proverb by choosing behavior which the proverb endorses as wise or by avoiding behavior which the proverb condemns as foolish.

Concrete applications of Proverbs 12:1 arise in situations where training takes place, especially that kind of training which involves reproof. Take the coaching of athletes, for example. Coaches are concerned not only to drill their athletes in correct techniques and strategies, they are also concerned to discern, reprove and correct defects in the athlete's performance of his or her sport. Other areas of application arise in military training, an art teacher's studio, a crocheting class conducted by the neighborhood recreation center, or a golfing clinic offered by the local country club. Those who love to "know how" will love the training that leads to knowing how, including the reproofs that come with discipline of any sort. Those who find reproof uncomfortable, damaging to their self-esteem and odious to the point where they reject it are identified in this proverb as stupid and certain to remain so, since they hate the very thing which will remove their stupidity.

The most important application of Proverbs 12:1 is the one which confronts you personally when you encounter reproof or submit yourself to training. To know in detail hundreds of examples of how this proverb applies is of no avail if you do not choose the wise path when it opens before you in your own experience. Learning to recognize the right path is only half the battle; choosing to walk on it is what gives success.

Topical Studies in the Proverbs
Organization of the proverbs by subject is practically non-

existent in the canonical text. In a few places some proverbs appear to be grouped according to a certain word, as in Proverbs 16:1-7 where each proverb mentions the word LORD. Proverbs 16:12-15 mentions the king in each proverb. Proverbs 26:1-11 speaks not only about the fool, but also employs emblematic parallelisms in most of its proverbs. Following them in 26:12-15 are four proverbs about the sluggard. Excepting such sporadic clusters of proverbs, most of the proverbs appear to be recorded almost randomly. In no case does a cluster of proverbs gather all the proverbs of the book on that one subject.

Efforts by Bible teachers over the years to discern some order in the arrangement of the proverbs have proven unconvincing. This has led to attempts by some to reorganize the proverbs according to subjects, attempts which are only partially successful. In one recently published reorganization of the proverbs by subject, Proverbs 12:1 is listed under three different headings: Discipline, Knowledge and Love. Proverbs 17:7—"Excellent speech is not fitting for a fool;/Much less are lying lips to a prince"—is listed under four headings: The Fool, Lying, Speech and Political Leaders. However, Proverbs 12:26—"The righteous is a guide to his neighbor,/But the way of the wicked leads them astray"—is listed only under the headings Friends and Neighbors, and The Righteous; it is not listed under the heading Guidance, even though the word *guide* and the notion of *leading astray* would seem to qualify the proverb for a listing under that heading.

The diversity of subjects which may be mentioned in any one proverb makes exhaustive reorganization difficult. And the almost kaleidoscopic applicability of some proverbs makes reorganization impossible. How can one catalog, for example, the applicability of Proverbs 22:3?

The prudent sees the evil and hides himself,
But the naive go on, and are punished for it.
There is no activity under the sun which cannot profit from

the advice of this proverb, and it is in their applicability that the proverbs prove most advantageous.

This does not mean, of course, that subject studies are impossible or fruitless. The classical themes of wisdom are not difficult to perceive in the proverbs. Very profitable studies may be pursued on such characters as the fool, the wise man, the simple, the righteous, the wicked, the scoffer, the sluggard, the friend, the king and even the Lord. Character virtues and vices are also edifying subjects—anger, self-control, greed, generosity, laziness, diligence, deceit, honesty, kindness, cruelty, love and hate. However, such subject studies will not exhaust the proverbs; they will only serve to open to you the vistas of wisdom.

Study Questions: Chapter Eleven

1. Assign each of the following proverbs to one and only one of the following subject areas: Home, Job, Money, Living with the Lord or Parenting. If a proverb appears to fit in more than one category, list it in the one which is most appropriate.

☐ He who trusts in his riches will fall,
But the righteous flourish like the green leaf. (11:28)

☐ A wise son accepts his father's discipline,
But a scoffer does not listen to rebuke. (13:1)

☐ The wise woman builds her house,
But the foolish tears it down with her own hands. (14:1)

☐ In all labor there is profit,
But mere talk leads only to poverty. (14:23)

☐ Better is a little with righteousness
Than great income with injustice. (16:8)

☐ He who gives attention to the word shall find good,
And blessed is he who trusts in the LORD. (16:20)

☐ A foolish son is a grief to his father,
And bitterness to her who bore him. (17:25)

☐ He also who is slack in his work
Is brother to him who destroys. (18:9)

☐ A brother offended is harder to be won than a strong city,
And contentions are like the bars of a castle. (18:19)

☐ Wealth adds many friends,
But a poor man is separated from his friend. (19:4)

☐ It is better to live in a corner of a roof,
Than in a house shared with a contentious woman. (21:9)

☐ The sacrifice of the wicked is an abomination,
How much more when he brings it with evil intent! (21:27)

☐ There is no wisdom and no understanding
And no counsel against the LORD. (21:30)

☐ He who tends the fig tree will eat its fruit;
And he who cares for his master will be honored. (27:18)

2. The following proverbs deal with wealth and poverty. Assign each of them to one and only one of the following cate-

gories: How to Get or Retain Wealth, How to Become or Remain Poor, How to Get Wealth *and* How to Become Poor.

☐ Poor is he who works with a negligent hand,
But the hand of the diligent makes rich. (10:4)

☐ It is the blessing of the LORD that makes rich,
And He adds no sorrow to it. (10:22)

☐ Wealth obtained by fraud dwindles,
But the one who gathers by labor increases it. (13:11)

☐ Adversity pursues sinners,
But the righteous will be rewarded with prosperity. (13:21)

☐ In all labor there is profit,
But mere talk leads only to poverty. (14:23)

☐ Abundant food is in the fallow ground of the poor,
But it is swept away by injustice. (13:23)

☐ A wicked man receives a bribe from the bosom
To pervert the ways of justice. (17:23)

☐ He who loves pleasure will become a poor man;
He who loves wine and oil will not become rich. (21:17)

☐ The rich and the poor have a common bond,
The LORD is the maker of them all. (22:2)

☐ He who oppresses the poor to make much for himself
Or who gives to the rich, will only come to poverty. (22:16)

☐ A faithful man will abound with blessings,
But he who makes haste to be rich will not go unpunished.
(28:20)

☐ A man with an evil eye hastens after wealth,
And does not know that want will come upon him. (28:22)

3. Proverbs 22:3 says:
The prudent sees the evil and hides himself,
But the naive go on, and are punished for it.

Give a concrete example of this proverb in each of the following five activities: (1) going on a picnic, (2) getting married, (3) buying a house, (4) looking for a job, (5) selecting a pet for the children. One example for each line of the proverb is sufficient.

CHAPTER TWELVE

The Whole Ball of Wax: Meditation from Start to Finish

SOLOMON TELLS US HOW TO DO anything and everything in Proverbs 21:5:

The plans of the diligent lead surely to advantage,
But everyone who is hasty comes surely to poverty.

Applied to the business of getting wisdom from the proverbs, this proverb directs us down one path and away from another.

The road to poverty is the one traveled on most rapidly. Similarly, some people attempt to pick up the proverbs of Solomon almost willy-nilly seeking an immediate solution to some personal problem. They rarely find what they seek. The almost random way in which the proverbs are arranged, the complex network by which any one proverb may have applications in diverse areas of living, the design of any one proverb by itself—all these factors conspire to ensure that the hastier the search for wisdom, the more meager the results will be.

The true road to wisdom will be slower insofar as it incorporates two things missed in the hasty search for wisdom: diligence in the search and a plan for how to proceed. Many of the proverbs were written with a conscious literary method. Therefore, being aware of this method will better equip you to unlock their meaning. The key elements used in composing the proverbs—parallelisms and figures of speech—provide a scheme for studying a single proverb in a systematic fashion.

A Plan for Studying a Proverb

The following steps are recommended for studying any proverb. In the beginning you should follow these steps rather closely. After several dozen proverbs have been analyzed according to the procedure, the study process will become almost habitual.

Step one: determine parallelism. The parallelism of a proverb is the most comprehensive literary feature it displays. All other elements in the proverb take their significance from the parallelism. After you identify the parallelism of the proverb, the other steps will follow according to the type of parallelism exhibited by the proverb.

If the proverb is a synonymous or antithetical parallelism, pair off all the corresponding elements in the two halves of the proverb as explained in chapters three and four. Be alert for asymmetry in antithetical parallelisms. When it is detected, supply in the pairing-off diagram the implied contrasts which the proverb is making.

If the proverb is an emblematic parallelism, write down the correspondences between the emblem and the caption of the proverb as described in chapter five. Also write down as many points of identity as you can between the emblem and the caption.

If the parallelism is synthetic, puzzle out the relationship between the two lines of the proverb. This will be very easy when the relationship results in the proverb's taking a particular literary form, as in proverbs of the form "better this than that." As necessary, refer to chapter six to review the various kinds of synthetic parallelisms and special steps to take in the elucidation of each.

It often happens with a beginning student that he or she cannot immediately discern the parallelism of a proverb. This is especially true when the novice tries to identify the particular subclass of synthetic parallelism. Sometimes the point of an emblematic parallelism is obscure. For centuries students have puzzled over and debated the tantalizingly elusive comparisons in Proverbs 30:18-19. Or it may happen that a proverb may make good sense initially with either of two differing parallelisms.

When such difficulties arise, you can do one of two things. First, you may defer deciding the nature of the parallelism until figures of speech are identified and elucidated. Often this will make clear what was obscure. Or you may find that the proverb may make good sense with either of two parallelisms. In this case there is no reason to suppose that this ambiguity is not deliberate and that the proverb you are studying is really two proverbs! You should then continue to study each of them in tandem with the other. If the parallelism remains opaque, then you may attempt to continue your meditation without knowing the parallelism. Or you may elect to put the proverb aside until you have gained further wisdom in the study of wisdom. This is often the most prudent course. There are still many proverbs which, though somewhat difficult, are within the range of any student. In the work of meditating on these proverbs which you *can* fathom, you will develop discernment and skill to successfully ponder more difficult proverbs. To stubbornly continue working with a very difficult proverb will only produce undesirable results—either fallacious solutions to the riddle of the proverb, or discouragement.

Step two: identify figures of speech. First, test the proverb for figurative language as described in chapter seven. Once figurative speech is detected, classify the figure(s) as either comparing figures or substituting figures. You can review how to elucidate comparing figures of speech in chapter eight and substituting figures in chapters nine and ten.

After identifying the figures of speech, you should attempt to express the sense of the figure in your own words without employing any figures of speech. You should not be dismayed to find that your own nonfigurative paraphrase of some figure results in an abundance of awkward words. Among the many virtues of figures is their efficiency in communicating information. By paraphrasing a figure in plain prose, you will come to appreciate the semantic power of figures and test your own understanding of figurative language.

Step three: summarize the proverb. After you draw out as many of the implications of the parallelism and the figures as you have time or skill for, you may feel as if the proverb has "unraveled" in disconcerting ways. At this point you should restate what appears to be the lesson or the principle of the proverb, using as few words as possible. Less than ten words is desirable. This step will require that you synthesize all the various insights which you have perceived in the previous steps.

Step four: particularize wisdom and folly. Write down in as clear and concrete a manner as possible what the proverb says about wise or foolish behavior. Many times the proverb sets before us a wise example to mimic. Other times a foolish action is set forth so we may learn to avoid it. Often both wise and foolish examples are portrayed in a proverb. Whatever the nature of the example set forth, carefully examine your own experience and the experience of others whom you have observed in order to find concrete examples of what the proverb speaks about.

Some proverbs do not set forth an example of folly or wisdom, but rather state a fact. An example of this kind of proverb is 22:2:

The rich and the poor have a common bond,
The LORD is the maker of them all.

In order to apply a proverb such as this it is necessary to discern what differences the truth of the proverb makes in the way we behave. Often other proverbs will serve to point the way. Proverbs 14:31, for example, helps in discerning the applicability of 22:2:

He who oppresses the poor reproaches his Maker,
But he who is gracious to the needy honors Him.

When you are seeking to particularize a proverb and to specify in concrete terms the wise and foolish behavior it shows, you should not worry much about being exhaustive. Rather you should concentrate on those areas of living with which you are most familiar, those situations and relationships in which you live and move. Your continual concern should be to discern where *you* are foolish, how *you* may choose and act in order to be wiser.

A Plan for Applying a Proverb

A fatal flaw in the study of anything is to confuse knowledge with action. James tells us that for "one who knows the right thing to do, and does not do it, to him it is sin" (Jas 4:17). James's warning, when made concerning wisdom, would be this: "One who knows the wise thing to do, and does not do it, to him it is folly." Something very near such an idea is expressed in Proverbs 26:7:

Like the legs which hang down from the lame,
So is a proverb in the mouth of fools.

There is, of course, a dimension to wisdom studies which involves knowledge, discernment and understanding. All these, however, are finally to be expressed in *deeds*, which are the ultimate expression of wisdom.

Keeping a wisdom diary can help you learn to study and apply wisdom to daily living. The diary is a notebook, preferably one which can have pages easily added or removed. The four steps for keeping a wisdom diary, listed below, should all be done within some recurring interval. Weekly intervals are recommended, as a week is brief enough to allow you to move quickly from study to the application of the proverb.

Step one: study the proverb. Study according to the plan previously described for a period not to exceed three days. Be sure to put some limit on your study so as to leave time during the remainder of the week for planning and living out the wisdom which your study has indicated. Keep the notes of your study in the notebook.

Step two: plan wise behavior. The key at this step is to look ahead for a situation where the proverb dictates some difference in what you might do. Look for problems of a recurring nature or situations in which you are failing—problems and failures to which the proverb speaks. You may want to select the proverb(s) you insert in the wisdom diary because of its obvious applicability to the areas where you need wisdom. Anticipate what you will do—or avoid doing—in light of the proverb you have studied.

Step three: behave wisely. Lady Wisdom, at the end of her invitation to the feast she has prepared (Prov 9:1-12), affirms that in the fullest sense the rewards of wisdom and the punishments of folly rest on the one who acts:

If you are wise, you are wise for yourself,

And if you scoff, you alone will bear it.

Proverbs 14:14 makes the same point:

The backslider in heart will have his fill of his own ways,

But a good man will be satisfied with his.

We are wise only as we choose the wise course, the wise path, or make the wise decision when the occasion arises.

Step four: evaluate your behavior. If you behaved wisely, note briefly in the diary what happened as a consequence. Be sure to note any additional insights into the proverb which you gained by attempting to apply it. If you failed to behave wisely, or if your "wise" behavior proved unsuccessful, try to describe why this happened. Write down how you plan to behave differently on the next occasion. Be sure to look for additional opportunities to apply the same proverb until you have succeeded in applying it.

The wisdom diary, kept individually over a span of months, provides a "drill" which can greatly facilitate your practice of meditation and application of individual proverbs. If you so desire, you can study and apply several proverbs touching on a single subject at the same time. The actual keeping of the diary is a technique which has proved very helpful in getting the beginning student of wisdom started. It should be attempted by every new student of the proverbs. It may be abandoned when it has served its purpose.

The method of study and application discussed above is especially fruitful when conducted in groups, such as family devotions or Bible studies. It invariably happens that penetrating insights into the meaning or application of a proverb will occur to one or two individuals of the group, insights which prove valuable to the other members. Brainstorming sessions around the study and application of proverbs are anything but dull if the participants share a minimal common understanding of how to unravel a proverb.

Getting Started

Confronted with the multitude of proverbs in Solomon's collection, you may feel somewhat lost as to where to begin. Reading through the book of Proverbs will only be of limited help in acquainting you with the contents of the book. Unfortunately, only a few topics or ideas may be entertained by the human mind at one time; ideally any "lesson" should have a solitary subject and precise, limited learning goals. Getting wisdom by reading the whole book of Proverbs is not much different from getting a liberal education by reading the *Encyclopaedia Britannica.* Indeed, reading the encyclopedia would be an easier way to acquire knowledge than reading Proverbs to acquire wisdom. In the encyclopedia, at least, your attention would be focused on one topic for as long as you read each article; in Proverbs your mind is presented with some new topic almost with every verse.

One useful way to be introduced to the raw material of the proverbs without destroying your attention span through an information overload is to attempt to classify all the parallelisms in chapters 10 to 31. The kaleidoscopic array of subjects in these chapters is thereby submerged under a single learning exercise—to classify all the parallelisms. While you are getting valuable practice in an elementary study technique in meditating on the proverbs, you are also being exposed to the raw material of the book.

If you would like to attempt this exercise, you can do so by ruling a page in your wisdom diary into five columns, each of them headed by the name of one kind of parallelism (synonymous, antithetical, emblematic, synthetic) and the fifth headed "undecided." You should take small portions of the book—perhaps a half to one chapter at a sitting—read each proverb in turn and jot down its chapter and verse in the appropriate column. After working through the book in this fashion, you may then wish to look once more at those proverbs in the "undecided" column. Then take each category of parallelism you have collected and apply further study techniques to them as appropriate. You could, for example, pair off all the corresponding elements between the lines of antithetical and synonymous parallelisms.

Some might fear that these exercises will prove dull and discouraging to further study. This seldom happens, however. These initial practice sessions are rescued from boredom by the continual novelty of new proverbs, by the challenge which each new proverb poses, and especially by the fresh insights which you gain in the process of acquiring and exercising new study techniques. Like calisthenics in the early stages of athletic training, these drills in studying proverbs can give new strength, agility and self-confidence in mining the wisdom of Solomon for yourself. Unlike calisthenics, these exercises are not mere repetitions of motions that go nowhere. Of course, you may choose to begin immediately to keep a wisdom diary. If so, it is important that you successfully master the exercises in the previous chapters.

Beginning the study and application of proverbs in a group setting can proceed exactly as with an individual, if a group can be assembled whose initial interest is in learning to study and apply proverbs. Afterwards, the group may elect a topic of common interest to study in a seminar fashion, each member of the group preparing and presenting one or two proverbs for discussion and evaluation.

The reader is directed to appendix 2 for examples of the study technique described early in this chapter. As you read these examples, keep in mind that each proverb is unique, and that the models in appendix 2 are only representative examples of how a study might proceed. Your own study may show differing emphases at various stages in the study in accordance with the properties of the proverb you are studying. No example of the wisdom diary is given. The steps in applying a proverb by this technique are simple and straightforward. No example can demonstrate what you need for the acquisition of wisdom—the willingness to put into practice what you have learned from the proverbs of Solomon.

[CHAPTER THIRTEEN]

When You Need Help: Various Aids to Study

AT THE END OF HIS TREATISE ON vanity in Ecclesiastes 12:11-12, Solomon advises those who would make wisdom their object of study:

> The words of wise men are like goads, and masters of these collections are like well-driven nails; they are given by one Shepherd. But beyond this, my son, be warned: the writing of many books is endless, and excessive devotion to books is wearying to the body.

The study of Solomon's wisdom will not only begin with the proverbs, it will not stray far from the proverbs. This advice has some element of paradox in it. The proverbs in many places counsel the seeking of counsel from others in a variety of areas (12:15; 13:10; 15:22; 19:20; 20:18; 27:19). And perhaps no book has spawned so many books about itself as the Bible. Yet, ironically, many people in Solomon's time and today have read dozens of books about the Bible but have never read the Bible itself.

There are dozens of books about the proverbs of Solomon and many more which take their themes and content from the wisdom of the proverbs. None of these books, however, have as their purpose to direct the reader to a fresh and original study of wisdom for himself. Furthermore, none of these books, indeed no book ever written—including Proverbs itself—can confer that success which only comes from choosing to walk in the wisdom you have learned.

The greatest single mistake in studying the proverbs is to turn too quickly to sources outside the proverbs for help. Books on bicycle riding or swimming are only limited help to those who have never ridden a bike nor swum. Most books on cycling and swimming are written for those already somewhat accomplished in these activities. In studying the proverbs, those who are most helped by books about the proverbs already have some accomplishment in studying them. Accomplishment in studying the Proverbs comes by studying the proverbs, not by reading books about them. As ever, we learn to walk by walking.

With this admonition in mind, you may wish to consult some of the works listed below as you study and apply the wisdom of the proverbs. These works are recommended with the following criteria: (1) they are confined, except for the commentaries, to works which will have utility in Bible study outside the proverbs, (2) they are readily available in most bookstores, (3) they are useful for the student who knows no Hebrew, and (4) they are relatively low cost.

General Reference
Douglas, J. D. et al., eds. *New Bible Dictionary*. 2d rev. ed. Wheaton, Ill.: Tyndale House, 1982. This is probably the most up-to-date one-volume Bible dictionary now available. It was written by an international team of over 150 scholars

and contains comprehensive articles on books and people of the Bible, notes on place-names, and studies of words and doctrines. A student with limited financial resources would do well to select this work out of all those recommended in this chapter.

Unger, Merrill F., ed. *Unger's Bible Dictionary.* Chicago: Moody Press, 1966. This is also an excellent one-volume reference work on the Bible, elementary biblical theology and the archaeological and historical backgrounds of the Bible text.

Tenney, Merrill C., ed. *Zondervan Pictorial Encyclopedia of the Bible.* 5 vols. Grand Rapids: Zondervan Publishing House, 1975. This five-volume encyclopedia is rapidly becoming the standard evangelical reference work of its kind. Hundreds of internationally renowned evangelical scholars have contributed a wealth of contemporary scholarship which takes into account most of the recent archaeological finds which bear upon the Bible. Its cost may be a factor to some, but it represents a sound investment for the serious Bible student.

Wright, Fred H. *Manners and Customs of Bible Lands.* Chicago: Moody Press, 1953. The table of contents and the Scripture index of this work limit its usefulness, but the content is very helpful for understanding many of the cultural allusions in the proverbs. This work is most helpful if you are able to read it in its entirety.

Concordances

Young, Robert. *Young's Analytical Concordance to the Bible.* Grand Rapids: Wm. B. Eerdmans, 1955. This concordance, rather than *Strong's Exhaustive Concordance of the Bible* (Abingdon), is more helpful in collecting proverbs according to some single word. *Young's Concordance* allows you to locate all the places where the Hebrew word occurs, even if that word is rendered differently in the English version from verse to verse. It is an invaluable reference work for word studies, which are often of great value in securing background material for understanding a proverb.

Voorwinde, Steven. *Wisdom for Today's Issues: A Topical Arrangement of the Proverbs.* Phillipsburg, N.J.: Presbyterian and Reformed Publishing Company, 1981. This small, inexpensive paperback does some preliminary concordance work for you, organizing the proverbs under more than fifty categories. While it gives a lot of a certain kind of help in a hurry, it is not exhaustive. You should not hesitate to gather additional proverbs under the categories Voorwinde has specified as it may seem appropriate; also, Voorwinde's categories are not all those which might be investigated. Still, it is a very handy and inexpensive help.

Torrey, R. A. *The Treasury of Scripture Knowledge.* Old Tappan, N.J.: Fleming H. Revell, 1973. The title page of this reprint from the previous century announces that the book contains "five-hundred thousand Scripture references and parallel passages from Canne, Browne, Blayney, Scott & others with numerous illustrative notes." The great usefulness of this work is its referring the reader from any one proverb to similar proverbs, passages in the Law of Moses, examples of the proverb from the Old Testament historical books or the New Testament Gospels, and to places in the New Testament where similar wisdom is taught or where New Testament authors build upon the wisdom in the proverb.

Versions

English translations of any portion of the Bible are the most basic kind of commentary available. The biblical authors wrote in Hebrew, Aramaic and Greek; translators, even those striving for the most literal rendering of the original languages, must make multitudes of interpretive judgments in expressing the ideas in the Bible through nonbiblical languages. Therefore, various English versions enable a student who does not read Hebrew to "see" the original text through different eyes. Where the English versions are in substantial agreement, you may safely assume there is little literary ambiguity in the original Hebrew text. Where English versions differ substantially, you will be alerted to literary or even textual problems in the Hebrew text.

The version which is best for the English Bible student is that version which leaves as many interpretive decisions as possible for him or her to make, especially in poetical books like Proverbs. It is also good to use a modern English version rather than the King James Version of 1611; advances in textual criticism, philology and archaeology since King James's day have made that version obsolete. This writer recommends the New American Standard Bible, as it presents the original Hebrew text with a minimum of paraphrasing.

You may also wish to consult other English versions for purposes of comparison. The Living Bible is very helpful in the study of Proverbs. It is *not* the English text on which to base the study and application of a proverb, for it is far too paraphrastic to represent anything other than Kenneth Taylor's interpretation of the basic sense of the proverb. However, in grasping the basic sense of individual proverbs, Kenneth Taylor was extremely adept. When you come to that place in your study where you try to restate the lesson or principle of a proverb in your own words, you would do well to check your paraphrase against the Living Bible.

Another version to consult is the New International Version, which tends to paraphrase more than the New American Standard Bible but less than the Living Bible.

Commentaries

Popular commentaries for the English Bible student are rare. Popular works tend to run toward exposition of the proverbs, doing for you what you would profit most from doing yourself; commentaries on Proverbs are mostly technical works which presuppose a working knowledge of Hebrew. In between these two camps are two commentaries which are helpful for the English student.

Kidner, Derek. *The Proverbs.* The Tyndale Old Testament Commentaries. Downers Grove, Ill.: InterVarsity Press, 1964. This work has two great virtues. First, the introductory material is excellent and will provide you with much useful information. You can easily expand a series of succinct subject-studies, and they serve as models which you can mimic in organizing your own subject-studies. Second, the comments on the individual proverbs serve primarily to illuminate obscure points without setting a finished interpretive conclusion before the reader. Guidance is given, but much room is left for you to pursue your own meditations. The moderate cost makes this an ideal commentary for the serious English student of Proverbs.

Cohen, A. *Proverbs.* Soncino Books of the Bible. Hindhead, England: Soncino Press, 1945. This is a Jewish commentary, including the Hebrew text, a translation by the Jewish Publication Society of America and a brief commentary of the same scope as Kidner's. Though the Hebrew text is provided, the commentary is written solely for the English reader. A sensitivity to Jewish culture and insights from Jewish sages make this a valuable companion to Kidner's commentary. But if you can only afford one, buy Kidner's.

The body of literature on Proverbs is immense. This book is adding a tiny increment to the books already available. All these books may prove somewhat helpful to one desiring to become wise. But after all the books have been written (and remember, Solomon says that will never happen!), there remains the book which Solomon wrote. He who would be wise will turn his ear and his heart to that book most of all, "to know wisdom and instruction, to discern the sayings of understanding" (Prov 1:2).

Chapter One

1. Proverbs: 1 Corinthians 15:32, 33; Ezekiel 18:2; Luke 4:23; Matthew 24:28; 1 Samuel 24:13.

Promises: Hebrews 13:5; 1 John 1:9; Isaiah 40:31; Romans 10:13; Exodus 20:12 (see below).

Laws/commandments: Deuteronomy 25:3; Matthew 5:44; Exodus 22:1; Leviticus 19:34; Deuteronomy 19:15; 2 Thessalonians 3:6. Exodus 20:12 is the fifth commandment of the Decalogue and is, therefore, a commandment. In Ephesians 6:2 Paul tells his readers that this is the first commandment with a promise, and then he isolates the promise in verse 3: "That it may be well with you, and that you may live long on the earth."

2. *Let us eat and drink, for tomorrow we die:* The concreteness of this proverb lies in its original context, a paradoxical merriment in the face of abject discouragement. It is generally applicable to any seemingly hopeless situation.

Bad company ruins good morals: This proverb is brief and very much to the point with an absence of colorful images or other figures. While the word *morals* seems to restrict the general force of the proverb to the realm of ethics, some reflection indicates that bad company will ruin more than a person's ethical values.

The fathers eat the sour grapes, but the children's teeth are set on edge: Concreteness is obviously this proverb's strong suit, brevity its weak one. Note how the increase in concretion over the previous proverb has the effect of also increasing the evident generality of its application. This proverb is appropriate in any situation where one "generation" errs and a later one suffers the consequences.

Physician, heal yourself: This proverb displays remarkable brevity and concreteness. Again, its generality of principle and diversity of application are enhanced by these characteristics. Notice that this proverb is almost never (in this author's experience, at any rate) quoted to physicians.

Wherever the corpse is, there the vultures will gather: Though not nearly so brief as the previous proverb, this one is especially graphic. The gruesome subject matter makes it all the more memorable. The wisdom principle—that some things are invariably linked together as causes and effects—makes this a widely applicable proverb. An extrabiblical proverb which makes the same point states, "Where there is smoke, there is fire."

Out of the wicked comes forth wickedness: The Hebrew original of this proverb is three words long. In English translation it loses this brevity and begins to sound platitudinous.

Chapter Two

1. Mental Proverbs: 11:24; 13:7; 15:30; 19:12; 26:4-5; 27:17, 19; 30:18-19.

Moral Proverbs: 11:17; 13:5, 18; 14:5; 15:3; 19:20, 26; 22:22-23; 29:11, 27. It is very rare that any proverb will have for its purpose only one of the two purposes of the proverbs. Proverbs which have a largely moral purpose may still have some intriguing and difficult figures of speech; and those proverbs which are manifestly riddles will have a moral lesson buried deeply in the dark saying. The proverbs identified in this question as having largely a moral purpose are those which define moral categories or affirm moral maxims with a minimum of figurative language; they are often in an imperative mood. Proverbs identified as having the mental development of the student in mind are so crafted as to require the solving of some riddle or the explication of some affirmed similarity before the moral lesson can be ascertained.

2. The background of the do's and don'ts in the Mosaic Law is a treaty, a contract, a covenant. The sovereignty of God and his authority to compel obedience to the laws have high profiles in the legal do's and don'ts of the Law. The "commandments" in Proverbs, however, have the flavor of the coach, the guide, the adviser. There is no treaty background to the moral instruction of the proverbs, at least as far as the wisdom teacher and the wisdom student are concerned.

Chapter Three

1. Synonymous parallelisms: verses 3, 6, 7, 11, 15, 18, 19, 20.

Antithetical parallelisms: verses 2, 4, 12, 14, 23, 24.

Neither synonymous nor antithetical parallelisms: verses 1, 5, 8, 9, 10, 13, 16, 17, 21, 22.

Proverbs 18:2 contains an ellipsis in the second line which, when supplied, makes the antithetical parallelism stand out strongly.

Proverbs 18:4 is a good example of the difficulty which can arise from figures of speech. It is hard to fathom how the two lines are to relate to one another until the sense of the figure of speech is determined. For the purposes of this exercise, 18:4 was classified as an antithetical parallelism because of the contrasting differences in the images set forth: deep waters versus shallow waters of a brook, the effervescent nature of the brook versus the still surface of a lake.

Proverbs 18:11 also employs a figure of speech to affirm something concerning the rich man's wealth. This proverb was classified as synonymous for two reasons: (1) the two images are predicated of the same subject, and (2) a high wall was a component part of a strong city at the time in history when this proverb arose.

Proverbs 18:14 employs a rhetorical question in the second line, the effect of which is to make a strong denial: *"No one* can bear a broken spirit." As the first line speaks of something which the spirit of man can endure, the parallelism is antithetical.

The other antithetical and synonymous parallelisms should be more or less clear from the previous chapter.

2. The King James Version translates 18:5 in such a way that the second line sounds like a consequence of the first line, namely, showing partiality to the wicked has the added consequence of overthrowing the righteous in judgment. The New American Standard Bible brings these two ideas more or less into synonymous relationship: by supplying the coordinating conjunction *nor* at the beginning of the second line, the proverb takes the form "A is not good, and B is not good." The only point of juxtaposing these two would be to affirm some sort of interchangeability between A and B. The translation of the New American Standard Bible is a synonymous parallelism; the translation of the King James Version is a synthetic parallelism (discussed in chapter six).

3. Proverbs 19:5, 9; 20:23 and 21:17 have one line which doubly negates some idea in the other line.

Proverbs 19:9 places in parallel *not going unpunished* and *perishing.* While it is not immediately clear that suffering punishment and perishing are interchangeable ideas, the latter might easily involve the former. In Proverbs 19:5, on the other hand, *not going unpunished* is parallel to *not escaping.* To see that the latter is a double negation of the former, we need to note that *going unpunished* would be equivalent to *escaping,* so that *being punished* is equivalent to *not escaping!* The phrase *not go unpunished* actually involves two negations—the word *not* and the prefix *un-.*

Chapter Four
1. Symmetrical: 11:15, 17; 13:3, 7; 14:11, 34; 18:23; 21:15; 28:5.
   Asymmetrical: 10:16; 11:3, 20; 14:2, 5, 25.

151

2.

10:16a	**10:16b**
the wages	the income
of the righteous	of the wicked
is life	(is death)
(is reward)	is punishment

11:3a	**11:3b**
the integrity	(the lack of integrity)
(the truthfulness)	the falseness
of the upright	of the treacherous
will guide them	(will lead them astray)
(will preserve them)	will destroy them

In English there is no easily recognized word which functions as an antonym for *integrity*, so *lack of integrity* is supplied in the above diagram as a suitable contrast. We might well have supplied *will not guide them* as a suitable contrast for 11:3b; however, as the treacherous are said to be destroyed, this suggested something more active. Therefore, *will lead them astray* seemed appropriate, especially when statements like Proverbs 11:5, 13:6 and 21:7 are considered.

11:20a	**11:20b**
the perverse in heart	(the not perverse in heart)
(not blameless in their walk)	the blameless in their walk
are abomination to the LORD	are His delight

This proverb is an example of how simple inferences can produce very helpful insights. From the diagram above we can see easily that the condition of a person's heart is displayed in the character of his behavior. Sin can be as much an aspect of our nature (compare Rom 7:18) as it is an aspect of our deeds. The second half of the proverb instructs us that mere behavioral modification is pointless. Those who are truly blameless in their walk have undergone a change in their nature.

14:2a	**14:2b**
he who walks in uprightness	(does not walk in uprightness)
(he who is not crooked	he who is crooked
in his ways)	in his ways
fears the LORD	(does not fear the LORD)
(honors Him)	despises Him

14:5a	14:5b
a faithful (truthful) witness will not lie	a false (unfaithful) witness speaks lies

14:25a	14:25b
a truthful witness saves lives (is faithful)	he who speaks lies (takes lives) is treacherous

Chapter Five

1. Making the correspondences in this proverb is difficult because three elements are mentioned in the emblem but only two in the caption. In the emblem are a pool of water, a face that looks into the water and a face that looks back. In the caption are *the heart of man* and *man*. Some have supposed that the dual mention of the word *man* is to correspond to the dual mention of the word *face* in the emblem, so that the point of the proverb would be something like "Look inward if you would know who you really are." However, the emblem, if considered concretely, indicates that even for knowledge of our external appearance, we must look away from ourselves into a reflecting medium such as water. Similarly, we must look away from ourselves to know our inner selves. The proverb points us to the heart of another who reflects back to us an image of ourselves. Those whom we know intimately are also those whose characters tend to reflect our own. We are accustomed to judge a person by the company he or she keeps. Proverbs 27:19 requires that we judge our own character in a similar fashion.

2. The emblems of Proverbs 25:26—a trampled spring and a polluted well —are similar in that both are sources of drinking water for the community which have been rendered useless. The emblems are different in the nature of the water source. Springs are close to the surface, wells are deep; springs occur naturally, wells are dug with much labor; spring water is running, sometimes almost effervescent, while well water is still; spring water is shallow, well water is deep.

If the righteous man can be symbolized by a spring or a well, evidently two kinds of righteous men are in view in this proverb, or perhaps a range of righteousness marked off by two extremes. The point of the proverb would seem to be twofold. On one hand, any righteous man who gives way before the wicked deprives the community of those things which they have come to depend on him for—wisdom, encouragement, leadership, example and so on. This much would be indicated by either emblem. Each emblem may indicate that recovery from the damage is variable according

153

to the nature of the individual righteous man. If the righteous character of the compromiser is shallow, effervescent, natural and uncultivated, as a spring's water, then recovery from such compromise can be foreseen. After time, the mud would settle, the trampled courses would find new channels and the water would run clear again. On the other hand, if his righteousness is the result of long labor, cultivation and expenditure of effort, then recovery is next to impossible. Polluted wells are irreparable or are cleansed very slowly, if at all. The compromising of a shallow righteousness is not nearly so calamitous as the compromise of long-established, cultivated righteousness.

3. Unlike most emblematic parallelisms which have multiple emblems, Proverbs 25:20 has two emblems which do not immediately appear to be members of the same class. Nevertheless, a little reflection indicates that in each action—taking off a coat on a cold day and placing vinegar on soda —a spontaneous and vigorous consequence results. The differences between the two emblems lie in the nature of the consequences of the action. In taking off a coat the unclothed person *contracts* physically in reaction against the cold, huddling, bending over, gripping the torso with the arms. In placing vinegar on soda an *expansive* consequence results as the chemical action of the soda and vinegar generates large amounts of carbon dioxide.

Again the point of the proverb would seem to be twofold. On one hand, singing songs to a troubled heart is certain to provoke a spontaneous and vigorous reaction. On the other hand, the nature of the reaction may be different. The person who is troubled may retreat spiritually and emotionally, as a person would physically when disrobed in the cold. Or the person with the troubled heart may explode in some strong emotional manner, as with tears or in anger. It is not impossible that both reactions might take place—a period of increasing emotional retreat concluded by a strong emotional outburst.

4. When an emblematic parallelism can be studied by resorting to a picture or perhaps the actual emblem itself, this can provide valuable insights into the proverb. "Cerebral cartooning" is surpassed many times by real cartooning. In Proverbs 11:22 an attempt to label the parts of the cartoon with the elements in the caption reveals how cunningly this proverb is constructed. There are two ways in which the cartoon may be labeled with the caption—the jewel may correspond to the beautiful woman and the pig her lack of taste, or the pig may be the beautiful woman and the ring her lack of taste. If we make an equation between the woman and the pig, then the basic point of the proverb would be that her beauty is really only a mirage and is wholly inappropriate to her character, even

as a jewel of gold in a pig's nose is wholly inappropriate. In this view the incongruity of the emblem is the essential point. On the other hand, if we identify the beautiful woman with the jewel and her lack of taste with the pig, then the point would be to emphasize not only incongruity but also the enormity of the character defect. The common man encountering a beautiful woman with no taste would probably be very impressed with her beauty, overlooking or failing entirely to notice her lack of taste. The view of the wise man, however, is set forth in this emblematic parallelism. When he considers a beautiful woman with no taste, he does not fail to note her beauty—there is, after all, the jewel of gold. But there is so little beauty and so much pig! The lack of taste looms far larger than the beauty in the wise man's estimation. Either way of understanding this proverb makes excellent sense; there is no reason to suppose that this ambiguity, or rather this dual message, is not intended.

Chapter Six
1. Classifying proverbs: 18:9; 21:4; 28:24. Proverbs 17:13 and 21:13 specify the consequences of some activity and are therefore synthetic parallelisms of the statement/consequence variety.
2. The demands which a poor man may make on friends and relatives often engender impatience in those who are looked to for benevolence. However, the bonds of family are normally stronger than those of friendship. If, therefore, the strongest bonds—those of blood—can be overcome by hatred, certainly those bonds which are weaker will succumb to the same fate all the more. It is important to recognize here that this proverb, like many others, affirms what is generally true in human behavior, not what is morally preferable. Where moral factors are considered, the proverbs come down squarely on the side of benevolence to the poor (see Prov 14:21; 17:5; 21:13; 22:22-23; 28:27; 29:7). Proverbs 19:7 is a warning, therefore, to the poor man whose plight has driven even his family away, that he cannot expect help from those who are tied to him by looser bonds than those of family.
3. Though the form of Proverbs 17:12 is not precisely that of the "better this than that" proverbs, its sense falls into that category of synthetic parallelisms. This proverb is true for at least two possible reasons (there may be more which you have discerned). A man meeting a bear can be damaged less than a man who meets a fool in his folly. Conversely, a bear can do no worse than a fool to the one who meets either of them. The proverb may also be making the point that one has more warning when meeting a bear robbed of her cubs than he has when he meets the fool pursuing his folly. With the bear there are obvious signs of danger, and therefore immediate

motivations to take flight. With a fool, however, the threat may not be so obvious. His folly may not be so manifest when a person first meets him, and so corrective action may be delayed until it is too late to avoid harm.

4. Statement/consequence: 14:26; 16:5; 28:9.

Statement/basis: 27:1; 28:21; 28:22.

5. Statement/purpose: 19:20; 27:11.

Statement/result: 17:11.

Either: 13:14.

Chapter Seven

1. *Buried deeply in the morning newspaper:* There is not enough mass in a normal morning newspaper to bury a full-grown man.

Grunts and mutterings informed Mary: To some ears this might signal a personification of grunts and mutterings as messengers or informants.

Wall of newsprint: John is not, in fact, holding a wall made out of newsprint.

The teakettle was boiling: The water in the teakettle was boiling, not the kettle itself.

Liberate her husband from the City News: John is not being held captive by the *City News.*

An idea slowly dawned: Ideas do not come to us over the eastern horizon in the morning.

Boiling water in hand: Mary had the teakettle in her hand, not the water itself.

As carefully as if she were walking on eggs: This phrase may be understood in a concrete sense without affirming nonsense, because it does not affirm that Mary is actually walking on eggs. Therefore, by the criteria discussed in the chapter, this phrase does not qualify as a figure of speech. However, it is so much like two other figures of speech that rhetoricians have named it a *simile* and have grouped it with the two other figures of speech (see chapter eight for further discussion).

The spout . . . took careful aim: Mary is the one aiming with the spout.

The peaceful and unsuspecting territory of John's lap: John's lap is not some pastoral countryside.

City hall woke up: Buildings cannot go to sleep.

Coming fully and warmly awake: John had not been asleep. Furthermore, wakefulness is not a thing which can have temperatures so as to be warm or cool.

2. Proverbs with figures: 12:18; 14:10, 15; 16:13; 17:7; 18:4; 20:8.

Proverbs without figures: 12:17; 13:11; 15:12; 17:2; 18:23.

Chapter Eight
1. Simile: 10:26; 18:8a, 19; 19:12.
   Metaphor: 10:15a, 29a; 16:24a; 18:9.
   Hypocatastasis: 16:23, 24b; 18:8b; 19:17.
2. The following features common to a rich man's wealth and a fortress are only a few of many that might be suggested:
(a) each is a source of protection
(b) each provides a base of operation
(c) each imposes its owner's authority merely by its presence
(d) each is overcome only by superior force or power
(e) each is inflexible to rapid change or movement
3. The words of a whisperer and a dainty morsel are alike in that—
(a) each is attractive
(b) each invites a consumer to sample it
(c) each is pleasant to the taste
(d) each develops an appetite for more
(e) consuming one leads immediately to consuming another and another
(f) each can be addictive
(g) neither is nourishing
(h) a steady diet of either produces personal damage
(i) the harmful effects of each are not immediately noticeable
(j) the harmful effects of copious consumption are a long time in going away

Chapter Nine
1. Proverbs in which *eye* is to be understood concretely are 10:10, 26; 16:30 and 23:29. In 12:15; 15:3; 23:33 and 28:22 *eye* is a synecdoche.
2. 14:15: *Steps* is a synecdoche for the prudent man's manner of living, construed here as being composed of many steps taken one at a time. By mentioning steps, this proverb highlights the fact that even the smallest details of the prudent man's life are scrutinized.
   13:25: *Stomach* is a synecdoche for the hunger of the wicked man. By specifying his stomach, the proverb holds out to us the idea that the wicked man, like the sluggard in Proverbs 21:25-26, is characterized by a ravenous appetite which is always in want because it is never satisfied.
   16:9: *Mind* (literally, *heart* in Hebrew) is a synecdoche for the man with the mind. *Steps* is the same synecdoche mentioned in 14:15 above.
   16:31: *A gray head* is a synecdoche for the aged man who has the gray head.
   19:20: *Days* is a synecdoche for the lifetime composed of days.
   19:29: *Blows* is a synecdoche for the punishment or judgment which comes to the scoffer in the form of blows.

Chapter Ten

11:11: *City* is a subject-predicate metonymy for the people who reside in the city, or perhaps the society located in that city. *Mouth* is a cause-effect metonymy for the *words* which the wicked speak.

12:6: *Blood* is very likely functioning here as two metonymies at once. First, it is a subject-predicate metonymy for violent death. However, an ambush is not a lying-in-wait for *blood* but a lying-in-wait for a *victim* in order to kill him. Therefore, *blood* as a metonymy for *murder* may also be understood as a cause-effect metonymy; instead of naming the victim, the proverb mentions the result for the victim.

14:1: *House* is a subject-predicate metonymy for *household*, its manners, customs, routines, character and traditions. *Hands* is a cause-effect metonymy for the *labor* or *deeds* which the woman performs with her hands.

15:25: Again, *house* is a subject-predicate metonymy for *household*. *Boundary* is a synecdoche for the widow's *property*. The outermost part of the property is mentioned in order to signify all that lies within.

16:30: *Winking the eye* and *compressing the lip* are both subject-predicate metonymies. For their significance, see Proverbs 6:12-15.

17:25: *Grief* and *bitterness* are cause-effect metonymies for the *deeds* of the foolish son which have as their effect the grieving and embittering of his parents.

25:5: *Throne* is a subject-predicate metonymy for the *reign* of the king, or perhaps his *judicial authority* (much as *bench* is today a metonymy for *judges*).

25:20: *Singing songs* is a subject-predicate metonymy for a *merry soul*, a happy-go-lucky spirit that is not troubled.

26:3: *Rod* is a cause-effect metonymy for *punishment* or *coercive influences*. Note that *whip* and *bridle* are also metonymies and are applied to beasts. The parallelisms point out the beastly nature of the fool when it comes to getting work out of him.

Chapter Eleven

1. Home: 14:1; 18:19; 21:9.
   Job: 14:23; 18:9; 27:18.
   Money: 11:28; 16:8; 19:4.
   Living with the Lord: 16:20; 21:17, 30
   Parenting: 13:1; 17:25.
2. How to Get or Retain Wealth: 10:22; 13:21; 17:23; 28:20.
   How to Become or Remain Poor: 13:23; 21:17; 22:16; 28:22.
   How to Get Wealth *and* How to Become Poor: 10:4; 13:11; 14:23; 22:2.
3. *Going on a picnic:* preparing a place to go if it rains rather than having

the picnic spoiled by unexpected weather

Getting married: anticipating and discussing budget expectations with a future spouse rather than waiting until after the marriage to discover irreconcilable differences

Buying a house: ordering thorough electrical, plumbing and appliance inspections before committing oneself to buy rather than finding expensive repairs cropping up in the first year of ownership

Looking for a job: inquiring closely of those already working for a business to see if they are pleased with their jobs rather than finding oneself with either unreasonable supervisors or unreasonable fellow workers

Selecting a pet: projecting annual food and medical costs for the new pet rather than finding out after it is purchased that the pet has become a strain on the family budget

The sample meditations on Proverbs 14:4; 20:20 and 25:20 are not set forth with the intent that you should slavishly copy them. For one thing, they record much of the raw thinking which might go into a normal meditation on a proverb, thoughts which would not normally appear on your own paper. Furthermore, these samples are done in a vacuum, compared to the context in which meditations on a proverb usually occur. For most students a meditation very soon takes on some particular significance and moves in a specific direction because of some need for wisdom peculiar to the student who is doing the meditation. The samples below lack that focus, indicating instead something of the diversity of application which each proverb may have.

Proverbs 14:4

Where no oxen are, the manger is clean,
But much increase comes by the strength of the ox.

Step one: determine parallelism. The word *but* in the English translation announces that the parallelism of this proverb is antithetical. Certainly there is a contrast between one element from each line: in the first line there are no oxen, while in the second line an ox is mentioned, though it is his strength which is specified. Otherwise, the contrast between the two lines is very asymmetrical. The implied contrasts are exhibited in the following diagram:

14:4a	14:4b
no oxen	(an ox)
clean manger	(dirty manger)
(no increase)	much increase
(no strength of an ox)	strength of an ox

A certain incongruity attaches to the word *manger*. The word *manger* in modern English (the KJV reads *crib*) signifies a box or trough in which animal feed is placed, and this meaning has been reinforced by nativity scenes in which baby Jesus is laid in such a trough. It is not quite clear what the proverb is getting at in mentioning a clean manger. *Unger's Bible Dictionary*, under the article "Crib" (the KJV's translation of the Hebrew word), notes that this word can mean "stall" and does mean this in Proverbs 14:4. Cohen's commentary also understands the word as an animal enclosure instead of the container where the animal's food is placed. "Where no oxen are, the manger is clean," because there is no animal to soil the stall. On the other hand, the dirty manger implied by the contrast of the proverb is a pungent image, especially to those who must regularly clean the soiled stall.

Step two: identify figures of speech. When the test for figures of speech is applied to the first line, no figurative language is evident; all the statements of that line can be understood concretely with no nonsense in the meaning. In the second line, however, the word *strength* is figurative; increase does not come directly or immediately from the ox's strength. Rather, the strength of the ox is deployed in doing work. The productive labor which the ox can do is what brings profit. *Strength* is a cause-effect metonymy for the *work* which is made possible by the strength of the ox.

For some students, this sense of the figure would be obscured if they did not know that oxen were common work animals in Hebrew society. Reference to the articles "Ox" or "Animals" in a Bible dictionary or encyclopedia would disclose this important piece of information. Wright's chapter on domestic animals in *Manners and Customs of Bible Lands* is also helpful in explaining the function of the ox in the agricultural economy of Israel.

Step three: summarize the proverb. Proverbs 14:4 is speaking from the realm of animal husbandry, but is this all it speaks about? Certainly a farmer whose strongest laborers are oxen would find wisdom in this proverb. However, does this proverb have any advice for the contemporary worker in an office building? The common characteristic of proverbial statements—to embody some general principle in a concrete example—is probably operating in Proverbs 14:4. To summarize the proverb requires that we abstract from it the general principle which it embodies.

When we look back to the parallelism diagram above, we see that Proverbs 14:4 presents two contrasting *pairs* of factors. On one hand, there is order but an absence of profitable labor; on the other, there is disorder but profitable labor. The point of this contrast would be to urge upon the reader a willingness to clean up the litter for the sake of the profit which labor brings. "Litter and labor go together" is one way of stating the principle or lesson of this proverb.

Checking with some of the reference aids confirms this sense of the proverb. The paraphrase of the Living Bible, for example, focuses more on the negative sense of Proverbs 14:4:

An empty stable stays clean—but there is no income from an empty stable.

Cohen's commentary sees Proverbs 14:4 as an "abstract thought presented by means of a concrete example." He explains the proverb as follows:

Having no ox is, from one point of view, an advantage because a man is then freed from attending to its care; but as against that there is the great advantage of having an ox for the provision of essential food. Consequently the disadvantage of having to look after the animal is far outweighed by the benefits which accrue from its employment in the field.

If you are a novice in studying the proverbs, you might find in these references the help you need if the general lesson of Proverbs 14:4 eludes you. If you are a practiced student and are able to penetrate to this sense of the proverb without resorting to commentaries, you will nevertheless find in the comments of others a confidence-building confirmation of your own meditation.

Step four: particularize wisdom and folly. Proverbs 14:4 gives us one particularization of the lesson it teaches. Folly is presented as the choice of an empty stable for the sake of its cleanliness with the resulting loss of profit from the ox which would sully the pen. Wisdom is presented as a willingness to clean up a mess with regularity for the sake of the profit which the laboring ox provides. Other examples of this proverb would be situations in which it is wise to choose labor with litter over an unproductive tidiness.

The head of a large legal firm first directed me to the lesson of Proverbs 14:4. This lawyer spent a large portion of his time in guiding, correcting, encouraging and admonishing the numerous paralegal technicians he had employed to perform the hundreds of hours of research required for his law practice. He also had to mediate personality conflicts among them. His "oxen" were the staff members, their "strength" was deployed in researching the law, and his "stable cleaning" was to keep them happy in their work and to help them avoid getting in the way of other workers with their own problems. Personnel managers and supervisors in many professions would profit from following the example of this lawyer who applied the farmer's methods and goals.

Discerning homemakers have also taken strength from Proverbs 14:4. Their "oxen" are the members of their families. Their spouses are employed in the business of providing food and shelter, and their children are in the business of growing up. The homemakers' "stables" are the households they manage as their families of oxen regularly and systematically disorder what they are continually cleaning up. Neither they nor farmers take any pleasure in the menial, repetitive work of stable cleaning; yet, if the oxen are well cared for, then their labor abounds to great increase for both the farmers and the homemakers.

Of course, there are the negative examples of Proverbs 14:4 in areas other than animal husbandry. Lawyers in single practice, for example, do not have the headache of managing office personnel. And neither are they able to handle the kind of lucrative law practice which only highly staffed law offices can manage. A woman also, if she is single or childless, does not have the frequent messes to clean up in the wake of husband and children. But neither can she bestow reward and success to a husband (Prov 12:4) nor ever know the joy of seeing the fruit of her womb mature under her care into righteous and wise adulthood.

It may happen that in areas other than animal husbandry the ox and the stable keeper are one and the same person. A carpenter, in order to build a piece of furniture, must create something of a mess in the process—scraps of wood and sawdust, paint and varnish splatters, and paintbrushes to clean. A tailor making a garment faces a similar situation—snippets of cloth and thread get scattered around; pins and needles, scissors and tape measures get laid about; all must be picked up and stored away after the garment is finished.

Again, if you have difficulty imagining areas in which to apply or concretize the proverb, a commentary may prove helpful. Kidner's comment on Proverbs 14:4 can point you in the right direction without doing your meditation for you:

> This proverb is not a plea for slovenliness, physical or moral, but for the readiness to accept upheaval, and a mess to clear up, as the price of growth. It has many applications to personal, institutional and spiritual life, and could well be inscribed in the minute-books of religious bodies, to foster a farmer's outlook, rather than a curator's.

The greatest profit from Proverbs 14:4 will come when you discover in your own life that place where the proverb directs you in a wise choice, so that you choose the productive labor even with its litter rather than settling for the ease of an unproductive neatness.

Proverbs 20:20

He who curses his father or his mother,
His lamp will go out in time of darkness.

Step one: determine parallelism. No comparison or contrast is made between the two lines of this proverb, so the parallelism is not antithetical or synonymous. The lamp going out presents something of a picture, but the point of bringing the lines of the proverb together does not appear to be the illustration of one line with the other. The extinguished lamp is not set before us as a picture but rather as an event which will transpire, so the parallelism is not emblematic.

By elimination, the parallelism of Proverbs 20:20 is synthetic. But what is the relationship between the two lines? First, observe that there are not two complete sentences juxtaposed in this proverb. The first line does not state an idea, but rather describes a person marked by a certain activity— cursing his father or his mother. This person is actually the subject of the complete sentence in the second line through the resumptive pronoun *his;* the point of the second line is not that some lamp will go out, but *this kind of man's lamp* will go out. It is not difficult to see in the construction of this proverb the idea that the lamp goes out *because* of the kind of man whose lamp it is. In other words, the relationship between the two lines is one of cause-effect in the broad sense.

Step two: identify figures of speech. Applying the test for figures of speech to the first line yields no figurative language; cursing one's parents is, sadly, all too capable of being understood concretely without nonsense. Applying the test to the second line, however, suggests that the lamp's going out is to be understood figuratively. If understood in the simplest concrete sense, we would have to imagine that the cursing man's lamp would go out at night if already lit, or perhaps it would not ignite. He would experience considerable inconvenience by the absence of light in his dwelling, of course, but this hardly seems a fate commensurate with his treatment of his parents. Moreover, we are left with the mysterious connection between his cursing and the extinguishing of his lamp. Something more seems intended by the lamp's going out, so the entire second line must be understood and interpreted as a figure of speech.

While we can detect this figure within the confines of the proverb, it is not possible to name and elucidate it within the boundaries of the two lines given. We may guess that the lamp's going out is possibly a metaphor or a subject-predicate kind of metonymy—the lamp's going out being an attendant circumstance of what is actually intended by the figure. Beyond this, we must look outside the proverb for understanding of the figure of speech. The nearest place to look is within the book of Proverbs itself for other references to *lamp*.

Recourse to *Young's Analytical Concordance* or the cross-references in *The Treasury of Scripture Knowledge* indicates that *lamp* occurs in the following places in Proverbs: 6:23; 13:9; 20:27; 24:20 and 31:18 in addition to

Proverbs 20:20. It is helpful to examine each of these proverbs for help in understanding the figure in 20:20.

Proverbs 6:23 is significant because it uses *lamp* in a figure which can be understood easily. It is also used in connection with one's relationship to one's parents in the exhortation which runs from verses 20-23:

My son, observe the commandment of your father,
And do not forsake the teaching of your mother;
Bind them continually on your heart;
Tie them around your neck.
When you walk about, they will guide you;
When you sleep, they will watch over you;
And when you awake, they will talk to you.
For the commandment is a lamp, and the teaching is light;
And reproofs for discipline are the way of life.

If *lamp* is a hypocatastasis in 20:20 for parental guidance, or perhaps living skills which are gained from parents, then Proverbs 20:20 is telling us that the man who curses his parents will find himself without the "light" he needs to live by, as this comes from his parents whom he evidently rejects.

Proverbs 13:9 is little help:

The light of the righteous rejoices,
But the lamp of the wicked goes out.

While the same figure appears in this proverb as in 20:20, there is nothing in 13:9 to explicate the figure for us.

Proverbs 20:27 makes a helpful equation:

The spirit of man is the lamp of the LORD,
Searching all the innermost parts of his being.

With this equation between the spirit of man and a lamp, we can infer that the lamp's being extinguished would indicate death. In other words, the one who curses his parents dies. Why and how he dies is not immediately clear in 20:20, but if basic living skills are learned from parents (6:20-23), then cursing one's parents could result in an ignorance of life and living which might prove fatal (1:32). This sense of the extinguished lamp is also supported by the parallelism of Proverbs 24:20:

For there will be no future for the evil man;
The lamp of the wicked will be put out.

Proverbs 31:18 gives an entirely different sense to a burning lamp. In the midst of a poem extolling the virtues of the excellent wife, we read:

She senses that her gain is good;
Her lamp does not go out at night.

Here we have almost the opposite statement from that recorded in 20:20b. In 31:18 the lamp's *not* going out at night is paralleled with the excellent wife's sense of accomplishment in her fruitful labors. We might infer that a lamp's going out at night would accompany a sense of personal failure or loss.

This inference would not be far from the mark. In *Manners and Customs of Bible Lands* (p. 27), we learn about the significance of light in a Palestinian household:

A lamp is considered to be the Palestinian peasant's one luxury that is a necessity. When the sun sets in the West, the door of his house is shut, and then the lamp is lit. To sleep without a light is considered by most villagers to be a sign of extreme poverty.... A late traveler looks to see a light in a house, and then he knows there is life there. To wish that a man's light be put out would be to wish him a terrible curse.

The excellent wife's sense of satisfaction in her gain is confirmed by the fact that she has light in her house throughout the night. If this is the background of Proverbs 20:20, then the lamp's going out would be a subject-predicate metonymy for the arrival of poverty.

To sum up: *lamp* in the book of Proverbs seems to be used figuratively for *life*—to indicate the spirit of man which enlivens the body (20:27), the skills by which one lives (6:23) or some minimum standard of living (31:18). A light's going out in time of darkness could indicate the onset of extreme poverty, the discovery that one is destitute of skills for living in some pressing circumstance, or even death.

Step three: summarize the proverb. In seeking to articulate the lesson of a synthetic proverb, it is often helpful to ask the question, Why? Why does Proverbs 20:20 link the cursing of one's parents with a life which results in impoverishment or even death?

The answer is given in Proverbs 6:20-23, cited earlier, and in several other places in Proverbs 1—9. From one's parents come the first and most basic skills for living. To curse one's parents indicates a profound rejection of parental instruction and the authority of parents which is exercised in giving that instruction. Wise parents not only teach a child but also enforce the lessons of life upon the child when necessary (Prov 29:15). A rejection of the parents will naturally carry over to a rejection of all that the parents have instilled in the child, as well as a rejection of what further lessons they may yet try to instill.

It is important to note that our basal attitudes to authority are formed through our relationship to our parents. Parents are the first authorities we meet in life, and the habits formed in relating to them carry over to all succeeding authorities. Success in living depends not only on what we learn from our parents *about* living, but also on how we learn to live *with* our parents. Leaving parental authority behind when leaving the home does not mean we leave authorities behind. There are always people in authority over us in the form of employers, government officials and finally God himself.

It is no coincidence, therefore, to find a promise attached to the fifth commandment in Exodus 20:12: "Honor your father and your mother, that your days may be prolonged in the land which the LORD your God gives you." Moses was alluding to this promise when he exhorted Israel to honor God and to obey him in Deuteronomy 11:18-21:

> You shall therefore impress these words of mine on your heart and on your soul;. . . so that your days and the days of your sons may be multiplied on the land which the LORD swore to your fathers to give them, as long as the heavens remain above the earth.

Why then does cursing one's parents bring a diminished quality of life? Because to curse the source of one's life and skills in living is to reject all further authorities upon whom one's life continues to depend.

Step four: particularize wisdom and folly. Proverbs 20:20 tells us it is foolish to curse our parents; this implies necessarily that it is wise to honor and bless our parents. We are helped in our understanding as we isolate concrete examples of wisdom and folly.

The Old Testament story of Ham's dishonoring of his father Noah is one example of the folly this proverb warns against (Gen 9:18-27). In the same episode Shem and Japheth exemplify sons who honor their father by refusing to look on his shame and by covering it from others' sight. Shem and Japheth find blessing, while Ham's line through his son Canaan is cursed and ultimately expelled from Palestine (Gen 10:15-20; 15:18-21; Deut 7:1-5; Josh 21:43). In Jeremiah 35 we find another instructive example of the blessing which comes upon an entire household as a result of honoring one's parents.

In our own experience we may have met those who seem always to be complaining and criticizing their bosses, the government, their teachers, their pastors, their doctors and anyone else who is any sort of authority in their lives. Very likely they also despise their parents and have developed this habit from childhood. The unhappiness of such people is not difficult to perceive, for it may take very concrete forms such as chronic employment difficulties and violations of the law. Wisdom for us will be to honor our parents so as to develop a pattern of respecting all others on whom our well-being depends.

Proverbs 25:20
> Like one who takes off a garment on a cold day, or like vinegar on soda,
> Is he who sings songs to a troubled heart.

Step one: determine parallelism. This proverb is easily seen to be an emblematic parallelism. It is somewhat unusual as an emblematic parallelism in that there is more than one emblem—taking off a garment on a cold day and pouring vinegar on soda. The question naturally arises, Are the emblems essentially the same or are they entirely different? This question was raised in the study questions in chapter five. You may wish to consult once more the answer to question three of chapter five in appendix 1 for further discussion on this point.

Step two: identify figures of speech. The entire proverb is constructed as a comparing figure of speech, a simile, which is the nature of emblematic parallelisms. In addition to this, however, there are two further figures of speech in the last line. *Heart* is a synecdoche for the person who has the heart. A "troubled heart" denotes a person whose heart is troubled, *heart* signifying the inner person, not the organ for pumping blood. *Singing songs* is very likely another figure of speech. If it is not, then those who never sing at all will escape the folly this proverb presents to the reader. But surely it is something more than the mere singing of a song which causes difficulty. Singing songs is a subject-predicate metonymy for a person who is merry of heart, who expresses his jolly spirits through singing songs. The last line of this proverb describes two people: one who is effervescing with good cheer, the other who is troubled to the very core of his being. The jolly person who directs his mirth toward the troubled soul is compared to the emblems in the first two lines.

Step three: summarize the proverb. The elucidation of the parellelism tells us the effect a merrymaker has on a troubled heart. Some further reflection tells us why Proverbs 25:20 is true. The troubled heart needs a garment, as it were, to cloak it from the chill of its anxiety. What it does *not* need is an irritant in the form of a merrymaker who only unveils the hurt which the troubled person experiences and provokes him to a sour foment. A non-biblical proverb tells us that misery seeks company. The proper remedy for the troubled in heart is solace, not songs.

Step four: particularize wisdom and folly. The interpersonal dynamic displayed in Proverbs 25:20 occurs frequently between married persons. Sometimes the husband, insensitive to his wife's moods, displays a happy-go-lucky spirit to his spouse, only to see her become cloudy and silent and then erupt in tears of angry frustration. Conversely, a cheery wife may greet her sorely vexed husband after a hard day's work and discover that her somber husband responds to her gaity with increasing indifference as he retreats into a newspaper or the six o'clock evening news on the television.

Wisdom, first of all, learns discernment of another's moods. After that, Paul's advice in Romans 12:15-16 is precisely aimed at the lesson of this proverb:

Rejoice with those who rejoice, and weep with those who weep. Be of the same mind toward one another; do not be haughty in mind, but associate with the lowly.

If we desire to help those who are vexed from their grief to move toward joy, we will succeed only as we first go to them in their trouble to share it and cover it. Afterward we may lead them to calmer and more joyful spirits. To "sing songs" to them is essentially a proud and insensitive stance. It demands that they who are troubled come to us who are not. Such demands, even though innocently made, strip away the protection the troubled heart is seeking and present an irritant which aggravates rather than soothes.